12 elegant and
inspiring tutorials for
the contemporary
cake designer

Bellissimo
WEDDING
CAKES

HELEN MANSEY

First published in April 2015 by
B. Dutton Publishing Limited, The Grange,
Hones Yard, Farnham, Surrey, GU9 8BB.

Copyright: Helen Mansey 2015

ISBN-13: 978-1-905113-52-1

Publisher: Beverley Dutton

Group Editor: Jennifer Kelly

Art Director/Designer: Sarah Ryan

Book publishing

Copy Editor: Frankie New

Senior Graphic Designer and Photography Stylist:
Louise Pepé

Photography: Rob Goves

Magazine publishing

Editor: Jenny Royle

Copy Editor: Adele Duthie

Senior Graphic Designer: Zena Deakin

PR and Advertising Manager: Natalie Bull

Fresh flowers by Eden Blooms, Surrey
www.edenblooms.co.uk

Wallpaper supplied by wallpaperdirect.co.uk

Printed and bound in Slovenia by arrangement with
Associated Agencies, Oxford

Disclaimer

The Author and Publisher have made every effort
to ensure that the contents of this book, if followed
carefully, will not cause harm or injury or pose any
danger. Please note that some inedible items, such
as flower stamens and cake dowels, have been used
in the projects in this book. All such inedible items
must be removed before the cake is eaten. Similarly,
any non food-grade equipment and substances, such
as non-toxic glue, must not come into contact with
any cake or cake covering that is to be eaten. Neither
the Author nor the Publisher can be held responsible
for errors or omissions and cannot accept liability for
injury, damage or loss to persons or property, however
it may arise, as a result of acting upon guidelines and
information printed in this book.

$\mathscr{I}$NTRODUCTION

This book contains a contemporary collection of 12 wedding cake projects, ranging from one tier to five. I've tried to cover a whole host of techniques but the main difference between this book and many others is that it reveals the secret to achieving sharp-edged cakes. This technique will take your cakes to the next level, giving them a clean, elegant and professional finish.

I first discovered the sharp-edged technique a few years ago, after coming across some cake designs from Australia where this style originated. Seeing how perfect the finish was, I was determined to achieve it on my own cakes. After much trial and error, I have now honed the technique and this book is the result of those years of research, which I want to share with you. I have also provided the recipes for my most popular cakes with suggested filling combinations – they have all been tried-and-tested by many brides and grooms, as well as hundreds of wedding guests.

It is clear that there has been a rise in popularity for lace on wedding cakes. Many of the cakes in this book feature lace in different forms using a variety of royal icing techniques. I have been fortunate enough to attend classes in cake artistry taught by the master of royal icing, Eddie Spence MBE, and have used the traditional techniques he taught me to create cakes with a contemporary twist.

Several of the cakes are also decorated with a whole range of different sugar flowers, as well as fresh flowers. The sugar flowers I make are quite stylised, emulating the shape and overall appearance of a real flower whilst complementing and coordinating with the cake.

I hope with the information I have provided you will gain the confidence to try the increasingly popular sharp-edged method for cake decorating. Clients often tell me their guests do not believe the wedding cake is real until they cut into it and I take this as the highest compliment. Once you master the technique, you will see the difference it can make to your cakes.

$\mathscr{D}$EDICATION

I would like to dedicate this book to my children Charlie, Harry and Daisy.

$\mathscr{A}$CKNOWLEDGEMENTS

I would first like to thank Beverley and Robert Dutton for their continued support. From our first meeting they agreed to put my Bellissimo Flexi Smoothers into production. They also gave me the chance to teach at Squires Kitchen International School, contribute to the award-winning title *The Art of Sugarcraft* and now write my own book. I feel very privileged and will always be very grateful for the opportunities they have given me.

The next person I would like to thank is Eddie Spence MBE. I was fortunate to spend a year attending Eddie's classes on cake artistry at Eastleigh College. Eddie is a wonderful artist, teacher and friend. I would always look forward to spending time in his company each week and will be eternally thankful for the skills he taught me.

I would like to thank the publishing team: Jennifer Kelly, Frankie New, Louise Pepé and Sarah Ryan for their hard work putting the book together. Thank you also to the multi-talented Rob Goves who took the beautiful photographs.

Thank you to Hazel Shaw from Eden Blooms for providing the gorgeous fresh flower arrangements in the book.

Writing this book has been a real family affair and I couldn't have done it without all the help and support they have given me.

Finally I would like to thank all the couples who have commissioned me to make a wedding cake for their special day. It is a real honour to be invited to contribute to someone's wedding day and seeing one of my creations as the focal part of their reception is a true joy.

CONTENTS

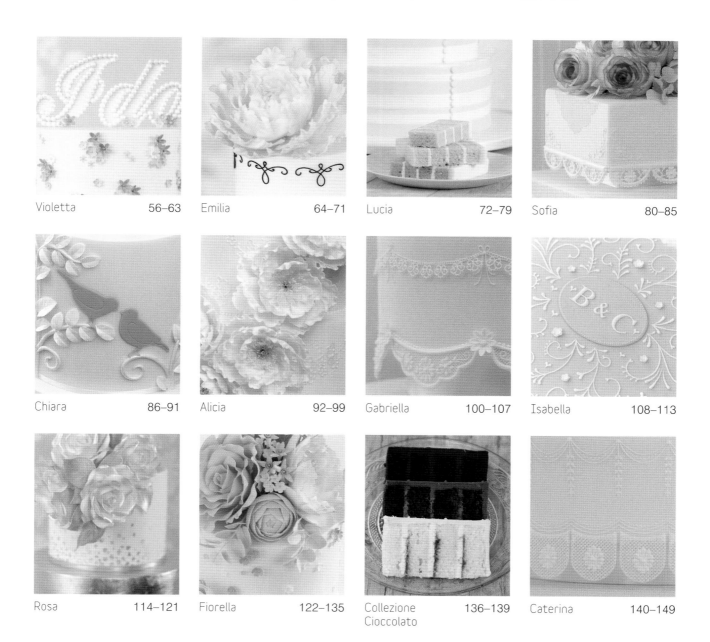

ESSENTIAL EQUIPMENT

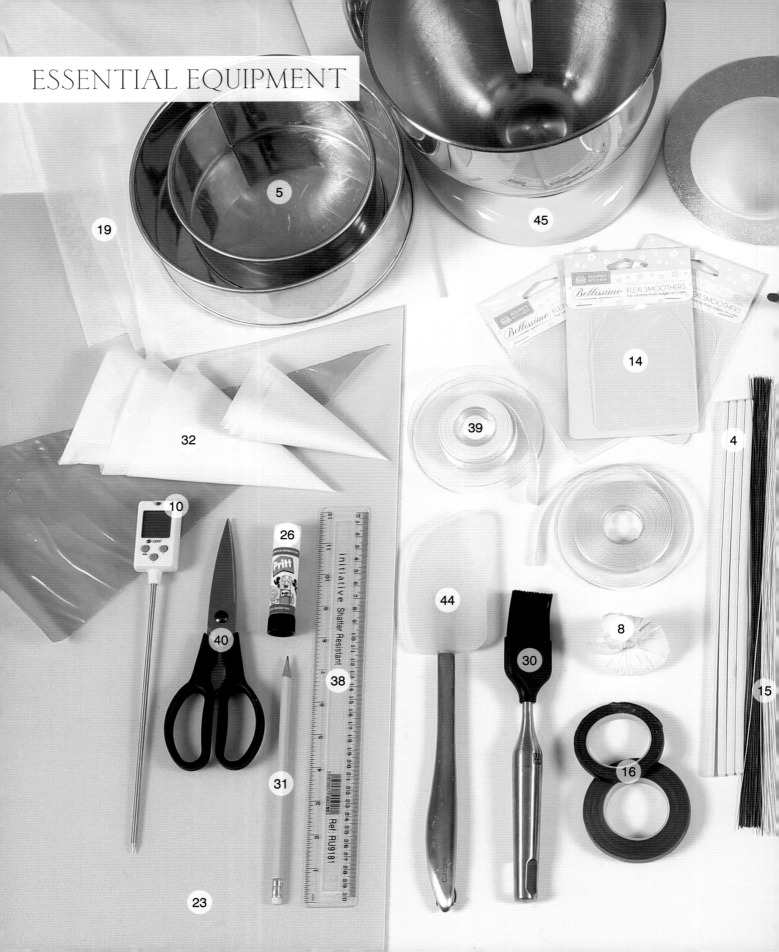

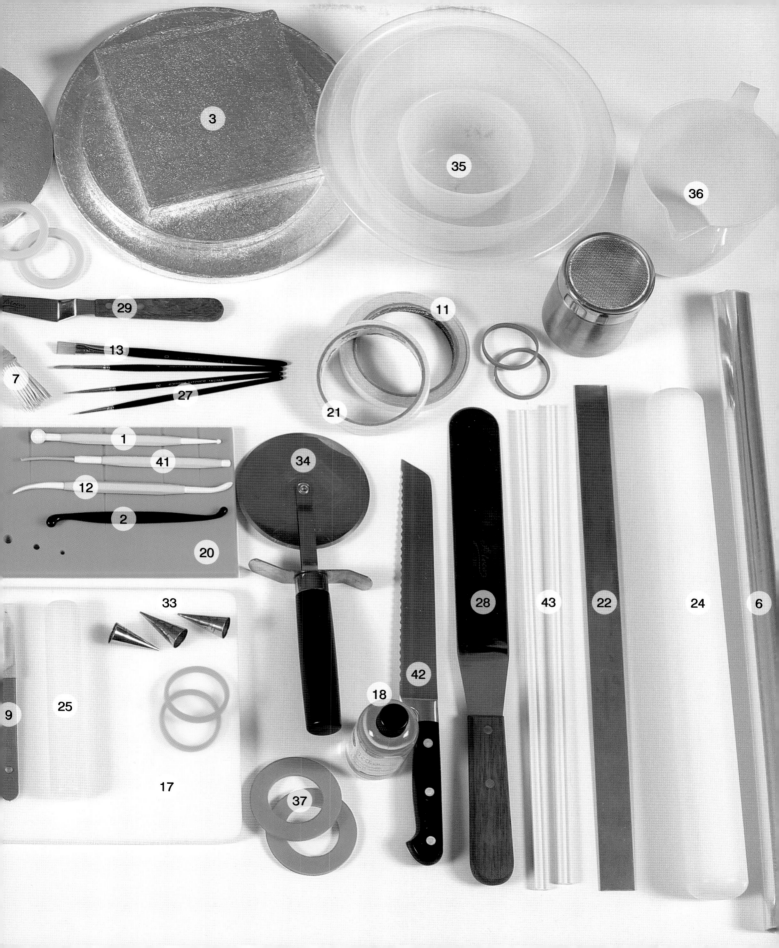

ESSENTIAL EDIBLES

ᴇSSENTIAL EDIBLES AND EQUIPMENT

When making a wedding cake, I know how important it is to have everything you need to hand before you begin in order to save you time and stress, especially when you have a busy schedule. The list below includes the same basic items you will need to achieve most of the wedding cakes in this book. Any other specific edibles or equipment are listed at the beginning of each cake tutorial. All of the items are readily available from sugarcraft suppliers, see page 160.

EQUIPMENT

1 Ball tools: large and small

2 Bone tool

3 Cake cards, boards and drums

4 Cake dowels

5 Cake tins

6 Cellophane

7 Cocktail sticks

8 Cornflour in a dusting bag

9 Craft knife

10 Digital thermometer

11 Double-sided tape

12 Dresden tool

13 Dusting brush

14 Bellissimo Flexi Smoothers: large, medium and small

15 Floral wires

16 Floral tape

17 Foam pad

18 Glaze cleaner (IPA)

19 Greaseproof paper

20 Grooved board/board with holes

21 Masking tape

22 Metal rule

23 Non-stick board: large

24 Non-stick rolling pin: large

25 Non-stick rolling pin: small

26 Non-toxic glue stick

27 Paintbrushes

28 Large palette knife

29 Cranked palette knife

30 Pastry brush

31 Pencil

32 Piping bags: paper and plastic

33 Piping nozzles

34 Pizza wheel

35 Plastic bowls

36 Plastic measuring jug

37 Rolling pin rings

38 Ruler

39 Satin ribbon

40 Scissors

41 Scribing tool (scriber)

42 Serrated knife

43 Spacers

44 Spatula

45 Stand mixer

EDIBLES

1 Edible lustre spray

2 SK Belgian Dark Chocolate Couverture

3 SK Edible Glue

4 SK Instant Mix Royal Icing

5 SK Professional Dust Food Colours

6 SK Sugar Florist Paste (SFP)

7 SK Fairtrade Sugarpaste

8 White vegetable fat

RECIPES AND BAKING CHARTS

As a wedding cake maker, I understand how important it is for the cake to taste as good as it looks, especially if it is being served as dessert. I regularly use the following tried-and-tested recipes to create cakes that are both delicious and suitable for decorating. I like to be able to offer my customers a wide choice, so I have included a selection of recipes for you to try.

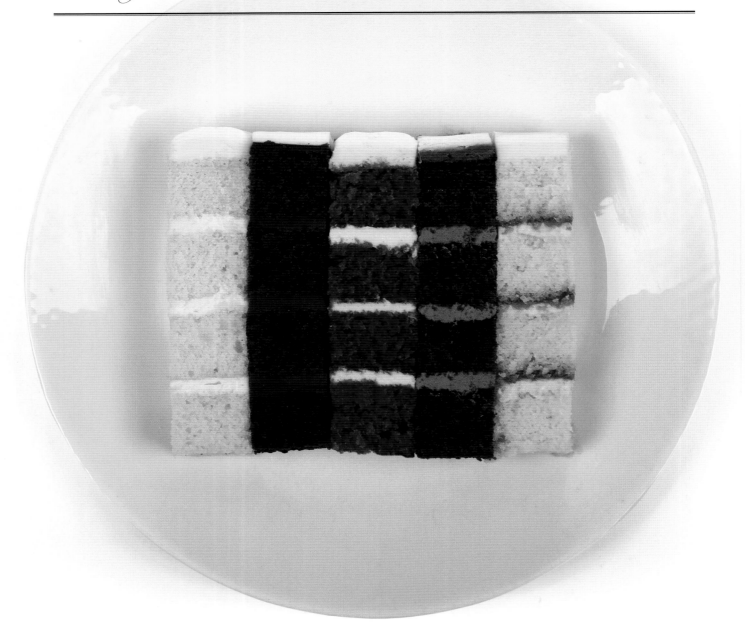

ℒINING A CAKE TIN

This method is a quick and easy way to line a cake tin. As I always recommend trimming the edges off cakes once they are baked to neaten them up, it is not necessary to spend a long time lining your cake tins.

1 Fold a piece of baking paper in half, making sure the area is slightly larger than the tin you are using. Place the tin on the paper and trace around it with a pencil.

2 Use scissors to cut around the shape approximately 5mm (¼") outside the line you have drawn. You should have two shapes that are slightly larger than the tin.

3 Put one piece aside and cut off 1cm (³/₈") from around the edge of the other piece. This piece will go on top of the cake when you bake it.

4 Take the end of a roll of baking paper and fold to make a rectangular strip that is the height of the cake tin plus an extra 2cm (¾"). Fold again to make enough strips to cover the sides of the tin. Cut through the folds with a sharp knife.

5 Grease the tin with a small amount of softened butter. Lay the larger shape you put aside earlier in the base of the tin.

6 Line the sides with the rectangular strips of paper. If you need more than one strip, grease the underside of the ends and overlap to ensure there are no gaps between the strips.

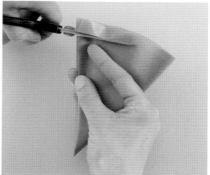

ℬAKING TIPS

To prevent the cakes from doming too much and to keep them moist, fill a deep baking tray with water and put this in the bottom of the oven while the cakes bake.

It is best to bake the cakes a day before you need them as this allows the crumb to firm up and makes it easier to cut them into layers.

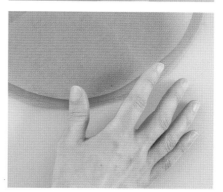

SPONGE CAKE

Simply add vanilla seeds or lemon zest to this sponge recipe for a cake that is deliciously light and full of flavour. I like to make my sponge cakes 12cm (4¾") in height with four layers of sponge and three layers of filling. I also use extra-fine flour as I find this results in a lighter, softer sponge.

Round	10cm (4")	12.5cm (5")	15cm (6")	18cm (7")	20.5cm (8")	23cm (9")	25.5cm (10")	28cm (11")	30.5cm (12")	33cm (13")
Square		10cm (4")	12.5cm (5")	15cm (6")	18cm (7")	20.5cm (8")	23cm (9")	25.5cm (10")	28cm (11")	30.5cm (12")
Butter, softened	175g (6oz)	225g (8oz)	285g (10oz)	340g (12oz)	450g (1lb)	625g (1lb 6oz)	800g (1lb 12oz)	965g (2lb 2oz)	1.08kg (2lb 6oz)	1.25kg (2lb 12oz)
Caster sugar	175g (6oz)	225g (8oz)	285g (10oz)	340g (12oz)	450g (1lb)	625g (1lb 6oz)	800g (1lb 12oz)	965g (2lb 2oz)	1.08kg (2lb 6oz)	1.25kg (2lb 12oz)
Eggs	3	4	5	6	8	11	14	17	19	22
Extra-fine self-raising flour	175g (6oz)	225g (8oz)	285g (10oz)	340g (12oz)	450g (1lb)	625g (1lb 6oz)	800g (1lb 12oz)	965g (2lb 2oz)	1.08kg (2lb 6oz)	1.25kg (2lb 12oz)
For vanilla sponge: vanilla pod	½	1	1¼	1½	2	2½	3	3½	4	6
For lemon sponge: lemon zest	1½	2	2½	3	4	5½	7	8½	9½	11
Baking time	50 mins	1 hour	1 hour 10 mins	1 hour 15 mins	1 hour 20 mins	1 hour 30 mins	1 hour 45 mins	1 hour 55 mins	2 hours 10 mins	2 hours 20 mins

TOP TIP

For sponge cakes 18cm (7") and larger, always bake the cake in a tin 2.5cm (1") larger than the cake size you require. This means you can trim off any dark crusts, leaving the cake the required size.

1 Preheat a conventional oven to 150°C/130°C fan/315°F/gas mark 1–2. Line the tins with baking paper and cut out an extra circle/square to go on top of each cake (see page 11).

2 Place the butter and sugar in an electric mixer and beat on a high speed until light and fluffy.

3 Stir in either the vanilla or lemon flavouring at this stage.

4 Lightly whisk the eggs in a jug and slowly add to the butter and sugar whilst mixing at a medium speed.

5 Sift the flour onto the mixture and stir in at a low speed. Scrape down the sides and bottom of the bowl with a spatula and mix again until well combined.

6 Spoon the mixture into the prepared tins and smooth over the top to level out the batter. Place a disc/square of baking paper on top of the cakes.

7 Place in the oven and bake for the required time. To check if it is baked, insert a skewer into the centre of the cake and if it comes out clean then the cake is ready.

8 Allow to cool in the tins. Once cold, turn out the cake and wrap it in cling film. Place in a cake box and store in a cool, dry place for up to two weeks.

ℳOCHA SPONGE CAKE

This is a lovely light, moist chocolate cake with a hint of coffee, making it a great choice for couples who want a delicious cake with a grown-up flavour.
Note: To make a 10cm (4") round cake, halve the recipe for the 15cm (6") round cake and bake for 45 minutes.

Round	12.5cm (5")	15cm (6")	18cm (7")	20.5cm (8")	23cm (9")	25.5cm (10")	28cm (11")	30.5cm (12")	33cm (13")
Square	10cm (4")	12.5cm (5")	15cm (6")	18cm (7")	20.5cm (8")	23cm (9")	25.5cm (10")	28cm (11")	30.5cm (12")
Butter, softened	100g (3½oz)	140g (5oz)	170g (5¾oz)	240g (8½oz)	340g (12oz)	410g (14¼oz)	510g (1lb 2oz)	580g (1lb 4oz)	640g (1lb 6½oz)
Caster sugar	190g (6¾oz)	240g (8½oz)	310g (10¾oz)	435g (15¼oz)	620g (1lb 5¾oz)	745g (1lb 10oz)	950g (2lb 1½oz)	1.05kg (2lb 5oz)	1.24kg (2lb 11½oz)
Eggs	2	3	4	6	8	10	12	14	16
Self-raising flour	50g (1¾oz)	60g (2oz)	85g (2¾oz)	120g (4¼oz)	170g (5¾oz)	200g (7oz)	255g (9oz)	290g (10¼oz)	340g (12oz)
Plain flour	135g (4¾oz)	180g (6¼oz)	225g (8oz)	315g (11oz)	450g (1lb)	540g (1lb 3oz)	675g (1lb 7¾oz)	765g (1lb 10¾oz)	900g (2lb)
Coffee granules mixed with hot water	2tsp: 20ml (¾fl oz)	1tbsp: 30ml (1fl oz)	4tsp: 40ml (1½fl oz)	5tsp: 50ml (1¾fl oz)	2tbsp: 60ml (2fl oz)	7tsp: 70ml (2½fl oz)	8tsp: 90ml (3fl oz)	3½tbsp: 100ml (3½fl oz)	4tbsp: 115ml (4fl oz)
Bicarbonate of soda	¾ tsp	1 tsp	1¼ tsp	1½ tsp	2 tsp	2½ tsp	1 tbsp	3½ tsp	4 tsp
Cocoa powder	50g (1¾oz)	60g (2oz)	85g (2¾oz)	120g (4¼oz)	170g (5¾oz)	200g (7oz)	255g (9oz)	290g (10¼oz)	340g (12oz)
Sour cream	170ml (5¾fl oz)	230ml (8¼fl oz)	285ml (10fl oz)	400ml (14fl oz)	570ml (1 pint)	680ml (1pt 3fl oz)	855ml (1pt 10fl oz)	970ml (1pt 14fl oz)	1.14l (2pt)
Baking time	*55 mins*	*1 hour*	*1 hour 10 mins*	*1 hour 25 mins*	*1 hour 35 mins*	*1 hour 45 mins*	*2 hours*	*2 hours 15 mins*	*2 hours 30 mins*

1 Preheat a conventional oven to 180°C/160°C fan/350°F/gas mark 4. Line the tins with baking paper and cut out an extra circle/square to go on top of each cake (see page 11).

2 Beat the butter and sugar together in an electric mixer on full speed until light and fluffy.

3 Lightly mix the eggs together in a jug with the coffee then pour slowly into the mixture, whilst mixing on half speed.

4 Sieve together the flours, bicarbonate of soda and cocoa and mix well.

5 Stir the dry ingredients into the egg mixture on slow and then add the sour cream. Scrape the sides and bottom of the bowl and stir again until well combined.

6 Spoon into the prepared tins and smooth over the top to level out the batter. Place a disc/square of baking paper on top of the cakes.

7 Bake in the oven for the time shown or until a skewer inserted comes out clean.

8 Allow to cool in the tins. Once cold, turn out the cake and wrap it in cling film until needed. Place in a cake box and store in a cool, dry place for up to two weeks.

𝒯OP TIP

For sponge cakes 18cm (7") and larger, always bake the cake in a tin 2.5cm (1") larger than the cake size you require.

ℛED VELVET CAKE

This red velvet cake is deliciously moist and the vibrant colour will be revealed once the cake is cut. For cakes smaller than 15cm (6"), bake the cake in a large square tin (see table) then cut it into quarters, level and stack.

For round cakes 18cm (7") or larger and for square cakes 15cm (6") or larger, bake four cakes in two tins, i.e. bake one batch after another. The table opposite gives quantities for each batch split between two tins, so remember that when you are shopping for the ingredients you will need to double the amounts. You can always mix up the second batch while the first is in the oven.

Round	10cm (4")	12.5cm (5")	15cm (6")	18cm (7")	20.5cm (8")	23cm (9")	25.5cm (10")	28cm (11")	30.5cm (12")
Square		10cm (4")	12.5cm (5")	15cm (6")	18cm (7")	20.5cm (8")	23cm (9")	25.5cm (10")	28cm (11")
Multiples of recipe	1 batch	1 batch	1 batch	2 batches	2 batches	2 batches	2 batches	2 batches	2 batches
Plain flour				175g (6oz)	225g (8oz)	340g (12oz)	410g (14¼oz)	510g (1lb 2oz)	580g (1lb 4oz)
Cocoa powder				1 tbsp	1½ tbsp	2 tbsp	2½ tbsp	3 tbsp	3½ tbsp
Baking soda				½ tsp	¾ tsp	1 tsp	1¼ tsp	1½ tsp	1¾ tsp
Baking powder	Bake 18cm (7") round cake recipe in 20.5cm (8") square tin	Bake 20.5cm (8") round recipe in 25.5cm (10") square tin	Bake 23cm (9") round recipe in 30.5cm (12") square tin	½ tsp	¾ tsp	1 tsp	1¼ tsp	1½ tsp	1¾ tsp
Salt				½ tsp	¾ tsp	1 tsp	1¼ tsp	1½ tsp	1¾ tsp
Caster sugar				225g (8oz)	315g (11oz)	450g (1lb)	540g (1lb 3oz)	680g (1lb 8oz)	770g (1lb 11oz)
Vegetable oil				125ml (4½fl oz)	175ml (6fl oz)	260ml (9fl oz)	315ml (11fl oz)	370ml (13fl oz)	430ml (15fl oz)
Buttermilk				125ml (4½fl oz)	175ml (6fl oz)	260ml (9fl oz)	315ml (11fl oz)	370ml (13fl oz)	430ml (15fl oz)
Eggs				1	1	2	2	3	3
Vanilla extract				1 tsp	1½ tsp	2 tsp	2½ tsp	3 tsp	3½ tsp
Red food colour				1 tbsp	1½ tbsp	2 tbsp	2½ tbsp	3 tbsp	3½ tbsp
White distilled vinegar				½ tsp	¾ tsp	1 tsp	1¼ tsp	1½ tsp	1¾ tsp
Coffee granules mixed with hot water				½tsp: 70ml (2½fl oz)	¾tsp: 100ml (3½fl oz)	1tsp: 140ml (5fl oz)	1¼tsp: 170ml (5¾fl oz)	1½tsp: 210ml (7½ fl oz)	1¾tsp: 240ml (8½ fl oz)
Baking time	45 mins	1 hour 5 mins	1 hour 20 mins	30 mins	35 mins	45 mins	55 mins	1 hour 5 mins	1 hour 15 mins

1 Preheat a conventional oven to 160°C/140°C fan/325°F/gas mark 3. Line the tins with baking paper and cut out an extra circle/square to go on top of each cake (see page 11).

2 Sieve the flour and cocoa powder into a bowl and mix well with the baking soda, baking powder, salt and sugar using a balloon whisk.

3 Mix the eggs, vegetable oil, buttermilk, vanilla extract, red food colour, vinegar and diluted coffee in a jug.

4 Pour the wet ingredients slowly into the centre of the dry ingredients, mixing constantly.

5 Pour the mixture evenly into the prepared tins and smooth over the top to level out the batter. Place a disc/square of baking paper on top of the cakes.

6 Place in the oven and bake for the required time. To check if it is baked, insert a skewer into the centre of the cake and if it comes out clean then the cake is ready.

7 Allow the cakes to cool in the tins, then remove and wrap in cling film until ready to use. Place in a cake box and store in a cool, dry place for up to two weeks.

TOP TIP

Although traditionally red in colour, you can use any food colour to make the cake match the wedding theme.

CHOCOLATE MUD CAKE

This chocolaty mud cake is decadent and rich – the ultimate cake for chocoholics.
Serve with cream for an indulgent dessert.

Round	10cm (4")	12.5cm (5")	15cm (6")	18cm (7")	20.5cm (8")	23cm (9")	25.5cm (10")	28cm (11")	30.5cm (12")
Square		10cm (4")	12.5cm (5")	15cm (6")	18cm (7")	20.5cm (8")	23cm (9")	25.5cm (10")	28cm (11")
Butter	90g (3oz)	130g (4½oz)	180g (6¼oz)	220g (7¾oz)	310g (10¾oz)	440g (15½ oz)	530g (1lb 2oz)	660g (1lb 8½oz)	750g (1lb10oz)
Dark chocolate	90g (3oz)	130g (4½oz)	180g (6¼oz)	220g (7¾oz)	310g (10¾oz)	440g (15½ oz)	530g (1lb 2oz)	660g (1lb 8½oz)	750g (1lb10oz)
Water	65ml (2¼fl oz)	95ml (3¼fl oz)	130ml (4½fl oz)	160ml (5½fl oz)	225ml (8fl oz)	320ml (11¼fl oz)	385ml (13½fl oz)	480ml (17fl oz)	545ml (19fl oz)
Coffee granules	2½ tsp	3½ tsp	5 tsp	2 tbsp	3 tbsp	4 tbsp	5 tbsp	6 tbsp	7 tbsp
Self-raising flour	50g (1¾oz)	75g (2½oz)	100g (3½oz)	125g (4½oz)	175g (6oz)	250g (8¾oz)	300g (10½oz)	375g (13¼oz)	425g (14¾oz)
Plain flour	50g (1¾oz)	75g (2½oz)	100g (3½oz)	125g (4½oz)	175g (6oz)	250g (8¾oz)	300g (10½oz)	375g (13¼oz)	425g (14¾oz)
Cocoa powder	20g (¾oz)	30g (1oz)	40g (1½oz)	50g (1¾oz)	70g (2½oz)	100g (3½oz)	120g (4¼oz)	150g (5¼oz)	170g (5¾oz)
Bicarbonate of soda	¼ tsp	¼ tsp	½ tsp	½ tsp	¾ tsp	1 tsp	1¼ tsp	1½ tsp	1¾ tsp
Caster sugar	190g (6¾oz)	290g (10¼oz)	380g (13½oz)	480g (1lb 1oz)	670g (1lb 7½oz)	960g (2lb 2oz)	1.15kg (2lb 3oz)	1.44kg (3lb 1½oz)	1.63kg (3lb 9oz)
Eggs	2	2	3	4	6	8	10	12	14
Vegetable oil	1 tbsp	4 tsp	5 tsp	2 tbsp	3 tbsp	4½ tbsp	5½ tbsp	7 tbsp	7½ tbsp
Buttermilk	45ml (1½fl oz)	70ml (2½fl oz)	90ml (3fl oz)	110ml (3¾fl oz)	150ml (5¼fl oz)	220ml (7¾fl oz)	265ml (9¼fl oz)	330ml (11½fl oz)	375ml (13¼fl oz)
Baking time	1 hour	1 hour 10 mins	1 hour 15 mins	1 hour 30 mins	1 hour 40 mins	1 hours 45 mins	1 hour 50 mins	2 hours	2 hours 15 mins

1 Preheat a conventional oven to 160°C/140°C fan/325°F/gas mark 3. Line two tins with baking paper and cut out an extra circle/square to go on top of each cake (see page 11).

2 Put the butter, chocolate and water into a pan and stir over a low heat until melted. Remove from the heat and stir in the coffee granules.

3 Sieve the flours and cocoa powder into a bowl. Stir in the bicarbonate of soda and sugar and mix well with a balloon whisk.

4 Mix the eggs, oil and buttermilk in a jug and pour slowly into the centre of the dry mixture, stirring constantly.

5 Add the chocolate mixture and mix until well combined.

6 Pour into the prepared tins and smooth over the top to level out the batter. Place a disc/square of baking paper on top of the cakes.

7 Place in the oven and bake for the required time. To check if it is baked, insert a skewer into the centre of the cake and if it comes out clean then the cake is ready.

8 Allow the cakes to cool in the tins, then remove and wrap in cling film until ready to use. Place in a cake box and store in a cool, dry place for up to two weeks.

RICH FRUIT CAKE

Many people have commented that this fruit cake is delicious and moreish, making it perfect for couples wanting a traditional wedding cake. Fruit cakes are best baked to a depth of 7.5cm (3"), any deeper than this then the sides, top and bottom can dry out due to the time the cake needs to bake in the oven.

Round	10cm (4")	12.5cm (5")	15cm (6")	18cm (7")	20.5cm (8")	23cm (9")	25.5cm (10")	28cm (11")	30.5cm (12")
Square		10cm (4")	12.5cm (5")	15cm (6")	18cm (7")	20.5cm (8")	23cm (9")	25.5cm (10")	28cm (11")
Sultanas	75g (2½oz)	110g (3¾oz)	150g (5¼oz)	190g (6¾oz)	260g (9oz)	375g (13¼oz)	450g (1lb)	560g (1lb 3½oz)	640g (1lb 7oz)
Currants	110g (3¾oz)	170g (5¾oz)	225g (8oz)	280g (9¾oz)	390g (13¾oz)	560g (1lb 3½oz)	670g (1lb 7½oz)	840g (1lb 13½oz)	1.43kg (3lb 1¾oz)
Raisins	75g (2½oz)	110g (3¾oz)	150g (5¼oz)	190g (6¾oz)	260g (9oz)	375g (13¼oz)	450g (1lb)	560g (1lb 3½oz)	640g (1lb 7oz)
Glacé cherries	15g (½oz)	20g (¾oz)	30g (1oz)	40g (1½oz)	50g (1¾oz)	75g (2½oz)	90g (3oz)	110g (3¾oz)	130g (4½oz)
Mixed peel	15g (½oz)	20g (¾oz)	30g (1oz)	40g (1½oz)	50g (1¾oz)	75g (2½oz)	90g (3oz)	110g (3¾oz)	130g (4½oz)
Brandy + extra for brushing	½ tbsp	1 tbsp	1½ tbsp	1½ tbsp	2 tbsp	3 tbsp	3½ tbsp	5 tbsp	5 tbsp
Lemon	½	½	½	1	1	1½	2	2	2½
Orange	½	½	½	1	1	1½	2	2	2½
Butter	75g (2½oz)	110g (3¾oz)	150g (5¼oz)	190g (6¾oz)	260g (9oz)	375g (13¼oz)	450g (1lb)	560g (1lb 3½oz)	640g (1lb 7oz)
Brown sugar	75g (2½oz)	110g (3¾oz)	150g (5¼oz)	190g (6¾oz)	260g (9oz)	375g (13¼oz)	450g (1lb)	560g (1lb 3½oz)	640g (1lb 7oz)
Black treacle	1 tsp	1 tsp	1½ tsp	1 tbsp	1 tbsp	1½ tbsp	2 tbsp	2½ tbsp	2½ tbsp
Eggs	1	2	2	3	4	6	7	9	10
Plain flour	90g (3oz)	140g (5oz)	190g (6¾oz)	235g (8¼oz)	330g (11½oz)	470g (1lb ½oz)	560g (1lb 3½oz)	700g (1lb 8¾oz)	800g (1lb 12oz)
Mixed spice	¼ tsp	½ tsp	½ tsp	¾ tsp	1 tsp	1¼ tsp	1½ tsp	1¾ tsp	2 tsp
Nutmeg	Pinch	¼ tsp	¼ tsp	½ tsp	½ tsp	¾ tsp	1 tsp	1¼ tsp	1½ tsp
Cinnamon	Pinch	¼ tsp	¼ tsp	½ tsp	½ tsp	¾ tsp	1 tsp	1¼ tsp	1½ tsp
Ground almonds	15g (½oz)	20g (¾oz)	30g (1oz)	40g (1½oz)	50g (1¾oz)	75g (2½oz)	90g (3oz)	110g (3¾oz)	130g (4½oz)
Flaked almonds	15g (½oz)	20g (¾oz)	30g (1oz)	40g (1½oz)	50g (1¾oz)	75g (2½oz)	90g (3oz)	110g (3¾oz)	130g (4½oz)
Baking time	*2½ hours*	*3 hours*	*3½ hours*	*4 hours*	*4½ hours*	*5 hours*	*5½ hours*	*6 hours*	*6½ hours*

1 Line a tin with baking paper so that it extends over the tin by 2cm (¾") (see page 11). Wrap the tin with a sheet of newspaper folded three times and tie with string.

2 Wash the dried sultanas, currants and raisins in tepid water and dry with strong kitchen paper. Be careful not to soak the fruit; you don't want the fruit to absorb extra water. Place the fruit in a large plastic container.

3 Rinse and finely chop the mixed peel and cherries, then add to the washed, dried fruit.

4 Remove the zest from the lemons and oranges and store in a container in the fridge.

5 Squeeze the juice from the fruit and strain over the dried fruit. Add the brandy, stir and allow to soak overnight.

6 Next day, preheat the oven to 140°C/120°C fan/275°F/gas mark 1.

7 Beat the butter, sugar and treacle in an electric mixer at a high speed until light and fluffy. Add the reserved zest.

8 Lightly mix the eggs in a jug and pour slowly into the mixture while beating on a medium speed.

9 Sieve the flour into a separate bowl and mix well with the spices and almonds.

10 Stir the flour mixture into the bowl, while mixing on a low speed. Scrape the bowl with a spatula and mix again until well combined.

11 Spoon the mixture onto the dried fruit and mix well.

12 Spoon the mixture into the prepared cake tin and cover with a disc of baking paper.

13 Place on a few sheets of newspaper or a piece of cardboard in the oven to protect the bottom of the cake and bake for the time required. Make sure that the paper doesn't touch the element or the flame in the oven. To check if it is baked, insert a skewer into the centre of the cake and if it comes out clean the cake is ready. If not, return to the oven for another 15 minutes and test again.

14 Once baked, remove from the oven and brush liberally with brandy. The heat of the cake will help it to absorb the alcohol quickly which helps mature the cake.

15 Allow the cake to cool in the tin. Once cold, wrap in a layer of greaseproof paper then cover with cling film.

16 Place in a cake box and store in a cool, dry place for up to six months.

RECIPES AND BAKING CHARTS

19

SUGGESTED FLAVOUR COMBINATIONS FOR LAYERED CAKES

Cake	Syrup	Filling	Coating
Vanilla sponge (see page 12)	Vanilla syrup (see page 24)	White chocolate vanilla ganache (see page 30), Swiss meringue buttercream (see page 23) and raspberry conserve	White chocolate vanilla ganache (see page 30)
Vanilla sponge (see page 12)	Champagne syrup (see page 24)	White chocolate champagne ganache (see page 30), Swiss meringue buttercream (see page 23) and strawberry conserve	White chocolate ganache (see page 28)
Lemon sponge (see page 12)	Lemon syrup (see page 24)	White chocolate lemon ganache (see page 30), Swiss meringue buttercream (see page 23) and lemon curd (see page 22)	White chocolate lemon ganache (see page 30)
Mocha sponge cake (see page 13)	Coffee syrup (see page 24)	Milk chocolate coffee ganache (see page 30) and Swiss meringue buttercream (see page 23)	Milk chocolate coffee ganache (see page 30)
Red velvet cake (see page 15)	Vanilla syrup (see page 24)	White chocolate vanilla ganache (see page 30) and Swiss meringue buttercream (see page 23)	White chocolate vanilla ganache (see page 30)
Chocolate mud cake (see pages 16–17)	Sugar syrup (see page 24)	Dark chocolate ganache (see page 28)	Dark chocolate ganache (see page 28)

GUIDE TO THE NUMBER OF SERVINGS PER CAKE

The wedding cake projects in this book all come with a suggested number of servings but you can use these tables to help calculate the number of servings of any cakes you make. Generally a wedding cake is cut into coffee portions, however, if the cake is to be served as dessert the portions should be slightly bigger.

ROUND CAKES

Cake size	Coffee portion: 2.5cm x 2.5cm x 12cm (1" x 1" x 4¾")	Dessert portion: 5cm x 2.5cm x 12cm (2" x 1" x 4¾")
10cm (4")	10	5
12.5cm (5")	15	7
15cm (6")	22	11
18cm (7")	30	15
20.5cm (8")	40	20
23cm (9")	50	25
25.5cm (10")	62	31
28cm (11")	75	37
30.5cm (12")	90	45

SQUARE CAKES

Cake size	Coffee portion: 2.5cm x 2.5cm x 12cm (1" x 1" x 4¾")	Dessert portion: 5cm x 2.5cm x 12cm (2" x 1" x 4¾")
10cm (4")	16	8
12.5cm (5")	25	12
15cm (6")	36	18
18cm (7")	49	24
20.5cm (8")	64	32
23cm (9")	81	40
25.5cm (10")	100	59
28cm (11")	121	60
30.5cm (12")	144	72

Ombre Cakes

Having an ombre cake with different-coloured layers adds another dimension to a wedding cake and allows you to match it to the bridal colour scheme. The following method explains how to create a graduated ombre effect using any colour. Following the sponge recipe on page 12, you will need to make a cake mixture that is 1½ times your chosen tin size – this will give you enough mixture for five layers and a little extra to allow for trimming.

1 Preheat a conventional oven to 150°C/130°C fan/300°F/gas mark 2.

2 Line two 15cm (6") cake tins of your chosen size with baking parchment (see page 11).

3 Split the sponge mixture into five bowls. Add a very small amount of food colour to one bowl and mix in well. Repeat for the next bowl, adding slightly more colour. Repeat with the remaining bowls, adding a little more colour each time until you are happy with the graduation of colour.

4 Put the lightest and second lightest bowlfuls of mixture into each tin and bake in the oven for half the baking time required or until the cakes spring back to the touch.

5 Remove from the oven and allow to cool for a minute. Turn out of the tins onto a cooling rack.

6 Re-line the tins, add the next two consecutive bowls of mixture and bake as before. Repeat again for the last bowl.

7 Once all the cakes are baked and cooled, wrap them in greaseproof paper and cling film and leave to settle overnight.

8 Cut each of the cake layers to 2cm (¾") deep and assemble the cake following the method on pages 34 to 36. The darkest colour tier should be the base with the layers getting lighter towards the top of the cake. Allow to set overnight.

FILLINGS

LEMON CURD

When necessary I use good-quality, shop-bought conserves in my cakes and always sieve them first before use. However, to be economical, I have created a lemon curd recipe that uses just egg yolks. This means that if a recipe only requires egg whites, such as Swiss meringue buttercream, I can still make use of the leftover yolks.

INGREDIENTS

2 large egg yolks

75g (2½oz) caster sugar

Juice of 1½ lemons (approx. 70ml (2½fl oz))

40g (1½oz) butter

❤ ❤ ❤

Makes approx. 200g (7oz)/enough to fill a 20.5cm (8") cake

❤ ❤ ❤

---

1 Whisk together the egg yolks and half of the sugar in a bowl, then set aside.

2 Place the remaining sugar, lemon juice and butter in a saucepan and stir over a medium heat. Bring to a simmer then remove from the heat.

3 Whilst whisking the egg mixture, pour the hot mixture onto it in a slow stream.

4 Once the ingredients are all combined, pour the mixture into the saucepan and return to the heat.

5 Whisk constantly until the mixture begins to boil: it should have thickened slightly. Remove from the heat.

6 Place a sieve over a small bowl and strain the curd.

7 Place a piece of cling film directly onto the surface of the curd and allow to cool to room temperature. Once cool, transfer to the fridge for approximately 30 minutes.

8 Store in the refrigerator for up to two weeks.

$\mathscr{S}$WISS MERINGUE BUTTERCREAM

For sponge cakes, I like to use a mixture of ganache and Swiss meringue buttercream to create a delicious filling that is lighter than using ganache on its own. To achieve this I mix one part ganache to one part buttercream. This carries the flavour of the ganache through the cake and helps to stabilise the Swiss meringue buttercream in warm temperatures.

INGREDIENTS

2 (approx. 60g (2oz)) large, fresh egg whites

100g (3½oz) caster sugar

140g (5oz) unsalted butter, cubed and at room temperature

300g (10½oz) ganache (see page 28)

Makes 600g (1lb 5¼oz)

1 Ensure the bowl of your electric mixer is clean and grease-free. Put the egg whites and sugar in the bowl and place over a pan of barely simmering hot water. Allow to simmer, whisking gently until the temperature reaches 70°C (160°F). Keep the mixture at this temperature for two minutes then remove from the heat.

$\mathscr{T}$OP TIP

Cooking the egg white until it reaches 70°C and maintaining that temperature for two minutes will ensure that any harmful bacteria is destroyed. If you don't have a thermometer, ensure the sugar is completely dissolved and the egg whites are hot.

2 Transfer the bowl to the mixer and use the whisk attachment to whip the meringue on high speed until it is thick, glossy and the bottom of the bowl feels neutral to the touch (this takes at least 10 minutes). Only add the butter when the bottom of the bowl doesn't feel warm anymore.

3 Switch over to the paddle attachment and add the butter cubes individually with the mixer on a low speed until fully incorporated with a silky smooth texture. It will curdle to start with but keep mixing until it eventually becomes smooth. If the mixture is too runny, refrigerate for about 15 minutes then continue mixing with the paddle attachment until it comes together.

4 To combine with the ganache, soften the ganache in the microwave until it has the consistency of smooth peanut butter. You may need to use the stick blender to help with this.

5 Add a spoonful of Swiss meringue buttercream to the ganache and mix in. Continue adding one spoonful at a time until you have a mixture that is one part ganache and one part buttercream. Mix with a stick blender if there are any lumps.

6 Once cool, store in the refrigerator for up to two weeks. Leave the buttercream out of the fridge overnight if you are planning to use it the next day.

$\mathscr{T}$OP TIP

To use the Swiss meringue buttercream as a cake filling, pipe a dam of ganache around the edge of each layer and fill in with the chocolaty buttercream (see page 38).

Sugar Syrup

Once the cakes are trimmed and layered, brush sugar syrup lightly over each layer – this helps to keep the cakes moist and adds additional flavour.

INGREDIENTS

100ml (3½fl oz) water

100g (3½oz) sugar

Makes 200ml (7fl oz)

1 Place the water and sugar in a saucepan over a high heat and stir until the sugar has dissolved and the syrup starts to boil. Pour into a bowl and allow to cool.

2 Store in the refrigerator for up to two weeks.

FLAVOUR VARIATIONS

Lemon/orange

Replace the water with freshly squeezed lemon or orange juice.

Vanilla

Add any scraped pods leftover from the vanilla sponge recipe to the saucepan. Allow 1 pod per 200ml (7fl oz) of sugar syrup.

Coffee

Add 1tsp of coffee granules to the syrup once removed from the heat.

Top Tip

Alcohol can also be added to syrups: as a guide use 25ml (¾fl oz) of alcohol to 200ml (7fl oz) of syrup.

Quantities of Fillings

The table below should be used as a rough guide for the amount of filling you need – you may wish to be more sparing with the syrup, especially for more moist cakes.

Cake	Amount of sugar syrup	Amount of Swiss meringue buttercream and chocolate ganache mixture
10cm (4")	60ml (2fl oz)	120g (4¼oz)
12.5cm (5")	90ml (3fl oz)	180g (6¼oz)
15cm (6")	120ml (4¼fl oz)	240g (8½oz)
18cm (7")	150ml (5¼fl oz)	300g (10½oz)
20.5cm (8")	210ml (7½fl oz)	420g (14¾oz)
23cm (9")	300ml (10½fl oz)	600g (1lb 5¼oz)
25.5cm (10")	360ml (12½fl oz)	720g (1lb 9¾oz)
28cm (11")	450ml (16fl oz)	900g (2lb)
30.5cm (12")	510ml (18fl oz)	1.02kg (2lb 4oz)

GANACHE

To achieve sharp edges on a cake you need a really firm foundation underneath the sugarpaste layer.

Conventionally, buttercream is used underneath the sugarpaste layer of a sponge cake – this is fine for round-edged cakes but unfortunately it does not provide a firm enough foundation for sharp edges and will not give you the perfect crisp finish this method does. The best foundation for sponge cakes is chocolate ganache made from either white, dark or milk chocolate. Because it is so important for all of the cakes in this book I have devoted this whole chapter to ganache – from how to make it to what can go wrong and how to fix it – and will explain all you need to know to achieve successful results.

What is ganache?

Ganache is quite simply a mixture of chocolate and cream which, if made correctly, has a delicious silky, smooth texture that melts in the mouth. Whilst combining two ingredients sounds very straightforward, in fact, ganache is a complex emulsion of fat molecules and liquid.

Which chocolate should you use?

I find using dark chocolate with approximately 54% cocoa solids is ideal. If the cocoa solids are any higher the ganache will taste bitter, any lower and the ganache will not set firm enough. For white chocolate ganache, the chocolate will need to have approximately 28% cocoa solids; for milk chocolate, it will need to have approximately 33% cocoa solids.

What cream should you use?

The ideal fat content of the cream should be approximately 35%. I use whipping cream which, in the UK, has a fat content of 38% so is the best cream to use. Double cream has a higher fat content which could cause the mixture to separate. Single cream has a lower fat content which would reduce the shelf life of the ganache and, because of its higher water content, would not taste as rich.

What quantities should you use?

For a firm ganache the quantities of chocolate and cream vary depending upon the type of chocolate you are using. For best results, the ratio of cream to chocolate is 1:2 for dark chocolate ganache. For white chocolate ganache, the ratio of cream to chocolate is 1:3$\frac{1}{3}$. The ratio of cream to chocolate for milk chocolate ganache is 1:2½.

Can you flavour ganache?

Ganache is a versatile filling that can be infused with a whole range of flavours. It is essentially the filling you find in a chocolate truffle, so think of your favourite in a box of chocolates and be inspired! Simply add the flavouring when you heat the cream, then strain before use.

Alcohol can also be added to ganache after heating. As alcohol is also a liquid, you need to reduce the amount of cream by the amount of alcohol added. As a guide, it is advisable to use a 1:5 ratio of alcohol to cream, e.g. for Limocello ganache use 50ml (1¾fl oz) Limoncello to 250ml (8¾fl oz) cream.

Should you add the cream to the chocolate, or the chocolate to the cream?

Always add the chocolate to the cream. This is the opposite advice to most recipes but the success of your ganache depends on which way the two ingredients are combined. Just recall what happens if you accidentally spill a liquid into chocolate as you melt it – the whole thing will seize into a big lump. The problem can be rectified by adding more cream, but it is best to avoid the situation in the first place by pouring melted chocolate onto the cream.

How long will ganache keep?

As a guide, ganache should keep at room temperature for approximately two weeks, which should give you around a week to decorate the cake and a week for it to be eaten. However, this guideline depends on the temperature you're working in. If you leave the cake set up in a very warm room, it would be advisable to tell your clients to eat the cake straight away as the heat will reduce the shelf life of the ganache.

Can I store ganache in the refrigerator?

Once you have made the ganache, it needs to mature at room temperature for 24 hours. If refrigerated, the fat crystals that form in the ganache will become unstable and, once brought back to room temperature, might not be firm enough to create sharp edges. Putting the cake in the refrigerator for a few minutes in between assembly stages will not be a problem, but once the ganache has been applied it needs to set overnight at room temperature. Ganache that has been allowed to mature and is not needed straight away can be refrigerated or frozen after this time; allow to defrost at room temperature before use.

$\mathscr{T}$HE ULTIMATE GANACHE RECIPE

In my quest for the perfect ganache, I have experimented with lots of different recipes and experienced many problems along the way.

The traditional method of heating the cream then adding the chocolate can be a bit of a lottery; sometimes it works but other times it can separate or become grainy. The microwave method of heating the cream and chocolate together does not produce a ganache with a very long shelf life because the cream is not heated to a high enough temperature to kill any bacteria present in the cream.

Deciding I needed to know more about ganache, I did a little more research and purchased *Chocolates and Confections* by Peter P. Greweling[1]. In this book Peter describes a method that uses tempered chocolate to consistently produce a stable ganache with a very smooth, creamy texture. Being slightly daunted by having to temper chocolate, it took me a while to build up the courage to try the recipe but I was delighted with the results once I did. I now use a variation of this method – which I describe overleaf – as the basis for all my ganache.

Chocolate contains six forms of cocoa butter crystals and only two of these, forms 5 and 6, are considered stable. Tempered chocolate is simply melted chocolate that contains the stable form 5 cocoa butter crystals. When you heat the chocolate to the required temperature, the unstable fats are melted but the stable fats stay intact, producing a firm, stable ganache.

This recipe is a little more involved than a traditional ganache recipe because the cream is brought to the boil then cooled, before being combined with the melted, tempered chocolate. You will soon discover it is worth the effort because the resulting ganache will be fully emulsified and have a very smooth texture once set.

$\mathscr{T}$OP TIPS

- Add the tempered chocolate to the cream, not the cream to the chocolate.

- Remove the cream from the heat as soon as it starts to boil to prevent the cream reducing and the ganache separating.

- Combine the ingredients at the required temperatures as quickly as possible. The faster you emulsify a ganache, the better the final texture.

- Don't over-mix – stop when it looks glossy.

- Pour into a large, shallow container to a maximum depth of 5cm (2") and leave to mature.

- Mature at room temperature, not in the refrigerator: 20°C is ideal.

[1] *Chocolates & Confections* by Peter P. Greweling (John Wiley & Sons, 2007). Copyright ©2007 by The Culinary Institute of America. All rights reserved.

GANACHE

TEMPERED GANACHE RECIPE

INGREDIENTS

Dark

1kg (2lb 3¼oz) dark chocolate

500ml (18fl oz) whipping cream

Milk

1kg (2lb 3¼oz) milk chocolate

400ml (14fl oz) whipping cream

White

1kg (2lb 3¼oz) white chocolate

300ml (10½fl oz) whipping cream

EQUIPMENT

Small saucepan

Microwaveable bowl

Large plastic bowl

Large, shallow plastic container

Spatula

Digital thermometer

Cling film

Handheld blender

**This makes enough for an
18cm (7") cake**

---

1 Place the chocolate in a bowl and heat in a microwave on full power in 20-second increments (use half power for white and milk chocolate). Stir between increments.

2 Once it is approximately ¾ melted, remove the chocolate from the microwave. Leave to stand and stir occasionally until all the chocolate is melted.

3 Meanwhile, heat the cream in a small saucepan until it comes to the boil. Immediately remove from the heat and pour into a large bowl.

4 Leave the cream to cool to 40°C for dark chocolate ganache and 38°C for white and milk chocolate ganache.

5 Check the temperature of the chocolate: dark chocolate should be between 32–34°C, white and milk chocolate should be between 28–30°C. If the temperature is too high, chop up a small handful of chocolate and stir into the melted chocolate to bring it down to the correct temperature.

6 When the two ingredients are the correct temperature, pour a third of the chocolate into the cream while stirring vigorously in the centre with a spatula to form an emulsion. Continue to stir outwards until all the cream and chocolate are emulsified.

7 The ganache may look like it is about to split at this stage, but add another third of the chocolate and keep mixing.

8 Add the final third and keep stirring until it has emulsified.

9 Mix with a handheld blender for about 10 seconds to fully emulsify the cream and chocolate. It should look glossy, similar to mayonnaise.

10 Pour into a large, shallow container and directly cover the surface with cling film. Allow to cool and set overnight at room temperature.

11 After 24 hours the ganache can either be used straight away, refrigerated or frozen. To soften, warm in the microwave in 20-second increments until it has the consistency of peanut butter. If necessary, use a handheld blender to smooth the ganache.

TOP TIP

To reduce the temperature of the cream quickly, place the bowl in a sink filled with cold water and stir until it reaches the correct temperature. Be careful not to splash any water into the cream.

GANACHE

BELLISSIMO WEDDING CAKES

FLAVOUR VARIATIONS

White chocolate lemon ganache

1 Add the zest of three lemons to the cream whilst you bring it to the boil.

2 When it has reached boiling point, remove from the heat and place a lid on the saucepan to prevent any evaporating and let the zest infuse.

3 Strain into a bowl after five minutes to prevent the taste becoming bitter.

White chocolate vanilla ganache

1 Add two vanilla pods and the scraped seeds to the cream whilst you bring it to the boil.

2 When it has reached boiling point, remove from the heat and place a lid on the saucepan to prevent any evaporating and let the pods infuse.

3 After five minutes, pour the cream into a bowl and remove the pods.

White chocolate champagne ganache

1 Bring 250ml (8¾fl oz) of cream to the boil.

2 When it has reached boiling point, remove from the heat and pour into a bowl.

3 Add 50ml (1¾fl oz) of champagne.

Dark chocolate orange ganache

1 Bring the cream to the boil with the zest of two oranges.

2 When it has reached boiling point, remove from the heat and place a lid on the saucepan to prevent any evaporating and let the zest infuse.

3 After five minutes, strain the cream into a bowl.

For orange liqueur ganache, omit 80ml (2¾fl oz) of cream from the recipe and add 80ml (2¾fl oz) of Cointreau after you have strained the cream into a bowl.

Milk chocolate coffee ganache

1 Bring the cream to the boil. When it has reached boiling point, remove from the heat and pour into a bowl.

2 Stir 1tbsp of coffee granules into the cream.

For coffee liqueur ganache, omit 70ml (2½fl oz) of cream from the recipe and add 70ml (2½fl oz) of coffee liqueur when you add the coffee granules.

Quantities of Ganache

The table below provides the amounts of ganache you will need for covering and filling cakes of different sizes.

Cake	Amount of ganache for covering	Amount of ganache for covering and filling, if not using Swiss meringue buttercream
10cm (4")	420g (14¾oz)	480g (1lb 1oz)
12.5cm (5")	630g (1lb 6¼oz)	720g (1lb 9½oz)
15cm (6")	840g (1lb 15oz)	960g (2lb 2oz)
18cm (7")	1.05kg (2lb 5oz)	1.2kg (2lb 10¼oz)
20.5cm (8")	1.47kg (3lb 5oz)	1.68kg (3lb 9¼oz)
23cm (9")	2.1kg (4lb 7oz)	2.4kg (5lb 6oz)
25.5cm (10")	2.52kg (5lb 8¼oz)	2.88kg (6lb 3oz)
28cm (11")	3.15kg (6 15oz)	3.6kg (6lb 12oz)
30.5cm (12")	3.57kg (7lb 14oz)	4.08kg (8lb 13¼oz)

TROUBLESHOOTING TIPS

Why is the ganache grainy?

It can be a problem if you over-mix the ganache once the emulsion has formed and started to cool, so you only need to use a handheld blender for a few seconds. As soon as the ganache looks glossy, stop blending. If you continue to mix whilst the ganache is cooling it can start to separate and will appear grainy.

To repair a grainy ganache, warm it to 32–34°C for dark chocolate and 28–30°C for milk and white chocolate. Stir to melt the fat crystals, then use the hand-held blender to disperse the fat. If this doesn't work, the ganache is too high in fat and you will need to follow the instructions on how to repair a separated ganache (see below).

Why is there oil floating on the top?

This means the ganache has separated and needs to be repaired (see below).

Why has the ganache separated?

When heating the cream it is essential to remove it from the heat as soon as it comes to the boil. If not, the water content will reduce and the cream will become too high in fat. A ganache made with a cream too high in fat will separate because the fat droplets are packed too closely together, causing them to coalesce and float to the surface.

How do I repair ganache that has separated?

Heat a little more cream to boiling point, remove from the heat and allow to cool to 40°C. In a separate bowl, put one spoonful of cream and one of the separated ganache. Mix vigorously until emulsified, then add another spoonful of ganache and mix again. Keep adding one spoonful of ganache at a time. If it looks like it will separate again, add another spoonful of cream.

Why are there lumps in the ganache when it was smooth when I made it?

This is most likely to happen to dark chocolate ganache due to the high ratio of fats in the mixture. If not cooled quickly enough, the finely dispersed droplets of cocoa and fats have time to merge together and create lumps. To prevent this from occurring, pour the ganache into a large, shallow container to a depth of no more than 5cm (2"). This exposes a larger surface area of the ganache and helps it to mature quickly and evenly at room temperature, ideally 20°C. If poured into a deep container, the ganache will not cool quickly enough. If the room temperature is higher than 20°C, it will take too long to set. On a hot day, leave the ganache to mature in the coolest part of your house, but not the refrigerator.

Why can't I use it straight away?

If you use the ganache straight away it could turn grainy. Stirring the ganache whilst it is cooling encourages the dispersed fats to merge together giving the ganache a grainy texture. Fresh ganache is also very soft and for sharp-edged cakes the ganache needs to be a peanut butter consistency. It needs time to mature to reach this optimum texture.

$\mathcal{B}$ASIC TECHNIQUES

$\mathcal{M}$AKING A CENTRING BOARD

By marking out a spare cake drum, you can use it as a template to help you find the centre of any other cake drum/board. This technique will help with the assembly of the cake and ensure that each tier is positioned centrally for a professional finish.

EQUIPMENT

51cm (20") square cake drum

Long ruler

Pencil

Electric drill with a 10mm (³/₈") drill bit

1 Using a pencil and ruler, draw a line diagonally across the board from corner to corner. Repeat for the opposite corners.

2 Find the central point and, working outwards, make marks along the lines at 1.5cm (½") intervals. Starting from the point that is 5cm (2") from the centre, write the size of the appropriate board next to the mark. To work out the correct board size, the distance from the centre will be the same as the radius of the board. For example, 5cm (2") is the radius of a 10cm (4") board, so you would write 10cm (4") next to the mark, and so on. Repeat along each of the diagonal lines.

3 Drill a hole in the centre of the board using a 10mm (³/₈") drill bit.

4 To use the board, place the cake board you wish to drill a hole through onto the centring board. Centre the board between the four marked points for the corresponding-sized board.

5 Whilst holding the cake board firmly in place, lift the centring board and insert a pencil in the drilled hole to make a central mark on the cake board. Repeat for the remaining boards, if required.

6 Drill a hole through the centre of each board using the marked points as a guide.

ℋOW TO MAKE A CAKE FRAME WITH A CENTRAL POLE

If you are making a cake that needs to be stacked before delivery to the venue, then I would recommend using this central pole technique to ensure the cake doesn't collapse or move about in transit. However, you will most likely need an extra pair of hands to deliver the cake because it will be very heavy.

I wouldn't recommend using a cake drum because they are made from cardboard and not strong enough, so you will need to use a circle (or square) of MDF instead. If you are making cakes up to 25.5cm (10") in diameter, you should be able to get pre-cut circles of MDF from craft shops. If you are making cakes larger than this, you can ask a local carpenter or search online for companies that cut MDF to size. As the MDF is thicker than a cake board, the central pole can be screwed into place rather than glued, making it more secure.

EQUIPMENT

Centring board (see opposite)

Electric drill with 16mm (¹⁰/₁₆") drill bit

Cake boards, one for each tier

Circle of 12mm (½") thick MDF, at least 7.5cm (3") larger than the base tier

15mm (⁵/₈") diameter wooden dowel rod, for cake decorating

Hacksaw

Sandpaper

Screw

1 Find the centre of each cake board and the MDF circle using the centring board and mark it on with a pencil.

2 Drill a hole in the centre of the base board for each of the cakes.

3 To work out the length for the central pole, add the combined height of the cakes then minus 5cm (2") so that the pole comes halfway up the top tier. For example, a three-tier wedding cake with tiers that are 12.5cm (5") high would need a central pole that is 33cm (13") long.

4 Cut the pole to the required length with a hacksaw, making sure to cut the end at an angle. This will help you push the

dowel through the cake. Sand off any rough edges.

5 Place the pole over the central point of the MDF circle and use a drill to screw the pole firmly in place from underneath the circle.

6 Wipe the pole and board with alcohol to sterilise them before use.

Important note: As MDF is not approved for food use, the cake should not come into contact with the board. Make sure to cover the board with sugarpaste before assembling the cake and always place the cake on a cake board before positioning it on the MDF base board.

𝒯OP TIP

To cover a cake drum that has a central pole attached, roll out the paste in the same way as for a normal drum (see page 44). Make a hole in the centre with the wider end of a piping nozzle. Slide your arms underneath the paste, lift it up then lower the paste carefully over the central pole, inserting it through the hole in the paste. Continue to cover the drum following the method on page 44.

BASIC TECHNIQUES

ℋOW TO GANACHE A ROUND SPONGE CAKE

An immaculate base layer of ganache is the key to creating impressive sharp-edged cakes. Unlike buttercream, you can create crisp, angular edges with ganache, giving the perfect foundation for a sharp-edged sugarpaste covering. The instructions below also explain how to layer, fill and crumb-coat a cake with ganache for a professional finish. If you prefer to fill your cakes with buttercream, see the method on page 38.

EDIBLES

2 sponge cakes (see page 12)

Chocolate ganache (see page 28)

Sugar syrup (see page 24)

EQUIPMENT

3 cake boards: 2 cake boards the same size as the cakes and 1 cake board at least 5cm (2") bigger

Piece of thin card, at least the same width as the cake

Ruler

Compass (drawing tool)

Pencil

Cake leveller

Turntable

Pastry brush

Small, cranked palette knife

Cake scraper

Metal rule

1 Measure the diameter of a cake board which is the same size as one of the cake tiers. Subtract 1cm (3/8") from this measurement and divide it by two to find the length of the radius. Set a compass to the radius measurement and use it to draw a circle on a piece of thin card: the circle should be 1cm (3/8") smaller than the diameter of the board. Cut it out with a pair of scissors. Repeat to make a template for each cake tier.

2 Trim 2mm (1/16") off the base of the cake with a serrated knife and discard. Set the cake leveller to cut 2.5cm (1") from the base and cut the first layer from the bottom of the cake. Put this layer aside and cut another layer to the same height. Cut the second cake into two layers in the same way. Place the card template onto each layer and cut around it to remove the excess from the edge of the cake.

3 Heat the ganache in the microwave in short bursts and stir well (see page 28): use full power for dark ganache and half power for white and milk. It is ready when the ganache is the consistency of peanut butter. If necessary, use a stick blender to achieve a smooth consistency.

4 Place the larger cake board (or set-up board) onto a turntable and spread some ganache over the centre of the board. Place a smaller cake board centrally on top and press down. Smooth a small amount of ganache over the smaller board.

5 Place one of the bottom cake layers centrally on the board, ensuring there is a 5mm (1/4") gap between the cake and the edge of the board. Brush the cake layer with a small amount of sugar syrup, then spread a 5mm (1/4") layer of ganache over the top of it. Place a second layer of cake on top, place a cake board onto the cake and press down firmly. Remove the cake board and repeat with the remaining layers of cake.

6 Brush the outside of the cake lightly with more sugar syrup. Omit this step for sponge cakes that are already quite moist, such as a chocolate mud cake or red velvet cake.

7 Use a cranked palette knife to spread a thin layer of ganache over the top and sides of the cake to seal in the crumb.

8 Place the cake in the fridge for five minutes to allow the ganache to set. Remove and spread a 5mm (1/4") thick layer of ganache over the top of the cake. Draw a metal rule over the ganache to smooth it out, then use a ruler to check the height of the cake is equal all the way around. Remove some ganache with the metal rule or add more ganache if necessary. Refrigerate for another five minutes or until the top layer of ganache is no longer tacky.

9 Brush the remaining cake board with cooled, boiled water, then place it on top of the cake with the foil-side down. Place a ruler against the top and bottom boards to ensure they are in line, then

BASIC TECHNIQUES

35

do the same with the side of a cake scraper and repeat at several points around the cake.

10 Use a cranked palette knife or a scraper to apply ganache liberally over the sides of the cake: the aim is to fill in the gap between the sides of the cake and the edge of the boards. Pull a scraper around the sides of the cake to remove any excess ganache. Fill any gaps with more ganache and scrape again until the sides are almost perfect.

11 Refrigerate the cake again for 5–10 minutes, then apply a final coat of ganache. Clean the scraper with warm water then, holding the set-up board in one place, turn the cake and run the scraper around it at the same time until you are back to the start point. Leave the cake to set at room temperature: this will take around an hour depending upon the temperature of your kitchen.

12 Run a paring knife around the edge of the top cake board so that it pops off. If it is stuck, use a cake leveller to help lift the cake board from the cake.

13 Press a sheet of kitchen roll on top of the cake to absorb any water droplets. If you find any air pockets on the top, fill these in with more ganache and use the metal rule to smooth over the top of the cake again. Leave any ganache that is overhanging the edges and let the cakes set fully overnight at room temperature.

14 Once set, hold a paring knife flush to the side of the top edge of the cake and run it around the cake to remove any overhanging ganache.

How to Ganache a Square Cake

1 Follow the instructions for ganaching a round cake up to step 10 (see opposite), but use square cake boards and a square template instead. Place the cake in the refrigerator for 10 minutes to firm up.

2 Spread some ganache on one side of each corner then scrape away any excess by holding the scraper horizontally at the base of the cake and scraping upwards. Refrigerate for five minutes, then apply ganache to the other side of each corner. Scrape away the excess in the same way and refrigerate again.

3 Spread a little more ganache over the sides and corners to fill in any gaps and scrape upwards again. Do a final scrape on each side. Leave any ganache that is overhanging the edges at this stage.

4 To finish, follow the steps for ganaching a round cake from step 12.

Top Tip

If you refrigerate the cake between applications it helps to achieve a sharp, square edge.

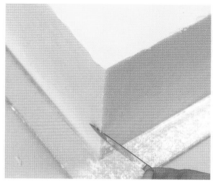

BASIC TECHNIQUES

HOW TO GANACHE A CAKE WITH A BUTTERCREAM FILLING

EDIBLES

Chocolate ganache (see page 28)

Swiss meringue buttercream and chocolate ganache mixture (see page 23)

Jam or lemon curd (optional, see page 22)

EQUIPMENT

Disposable piping bag

5mm (¼") round piping nozzle

1 Follow the instructions for ganaching a round cake up to step 4 (see page 34). Place one of the bottom layers centrally on the board, ensuring there is a 5mm (¼") gap between the cake and the edge of the board. Brush the cake layer with a small amount of sugar syrup.

2 Fill a disposable piping bag with soft ganache and a 5mm (¼") nozzle. Pipe a dam or border of ganache around the outside edge of the cake. Cover the rest of

the layer inside the ganache with Swiss meringue buttercream filling. Smooth over the buttercream with a metal rule so that it is level with the height of the ganache dam.

3 If using jam or curd, spread a thin coat over the next layer, approximately 5mm (¼") in from the edge. Turn the layer over and position onto the first layer. Finish layering and filling the cake, then proceed to step 6 for ganaching a round cake.

$\mathscr{H}$OW TO MARZIPAN A FRUIT CAKE TO CREATE SHARP EDGES

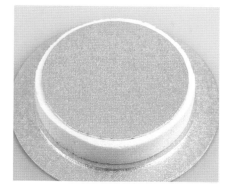

If you are making a traditional fruit cake for a wedding, you can still achieve the sharp-edged finish by using a layer of marzipan underneath the sugarpaste. I find fruit cakes are best baked to a depth of 7.5cm (3"), so I usually sandwich a separator between two cake boards to raise the height of the fruit cake to match the height of the sponges I make. Alternatively, you could bake two shallower fruit cakes, trim them to 5.5cm (2¼") high and sandwich them together with a layer of marzipan.

EDIBLES

7.5cm (3") deep fruit cake (see page 18)

Brandy

Apricot jam

Marzipan

EQUIPMENT

3 x cake boards: 1 x same size as the cake (A), 1 x 2.5cm (1") smaller than the cake (B) and 1 x 7.5cm (3") larger than the cake (C)

Polystyrene separator: 1cm (³/₈") smaller than the cake and 4cm (1½") deep

Sandpaper (optional)

Non-toxic glue

Piece of card

Cake leveller

Serrated knife

Pastry brush

Sieve

Rolling pin rings: 5mm (¼")

Non-stick rolling pins: large and small

Small, sharp knife

Cake smoother

Pizza wheel

Bellissimo Flexi Smoothers: medium

$\mathscr{T}$OP TIP

The polystyrene separator needs to be 1cm (³/₈") smaller in diameter than the cake, so you may need to use sandpaper to sand down the sides. Make sure you do this away from any food preparation areas, rinse off the dust and allow to dry before use.

1 Stick the board the same size as the cake (A) in the centre of the larger set-up board (C) with non-toxic glue, then stick the polystyrene separator centrally on top. Glue the smallest board (B) centrally on top of the separator and leave to dry.

2 Cut a round template from a piece of card that is 1cm (³/₈") smaller in diameter than the cake board underneath the separator (A). Trim the dome off the top of the fruit cake with a cake leveller or a serrated knife to create a flat surface.

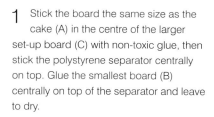

3 Place the template on top of the cake and trim down the sides with a serrated knife: hold the knife against the cake so that it is perpendicular to the board. You will find you are trimming more from the bottom of the cake than the top.

4 Remove the template and brush the top and sides of the cake with brandy. Leave to absorb for a few minutes.

5 Meanwhile, bring some apricot jam to the boil in a saucepan then remove from the heat. Sieve the jam into a bowl to create a glaze and brush it over the top of the cake.

6 Attach the rolling pin rings to the ends of the rolling pin and roll out some marzipan to 5mm (¼") thick and bigger than the fruit cake. Flip the cake over onto the marzipan and trim around the edge of the cake.

7 Brush some apricot glaze over the smallest board (B) and flip the cake back over onto the board so that the marzipan layer is on top. Smooth over the marzipan with a cake smoother. Brush the sides of the cake with apricot glaze, then brush over the separator.

*T*op Tip

Once you've brushed glaze over the separator, make sure not to brush over the cake again because you could transfer inedible flakes of polystyrene to the cake.

8 Roll a thin sausage of marzipan that is approximately the same length as the circumference of the cake. Wrap the sausage around the base of the cake to fill the gap between the cake, the bottom of the board and the separator.

9 Roll out a strip of marzipan that is slightly higher than the sides of the cake and slightly longer than the circumference. Roll up the marzipan around a small rolling pin, hold it up to the side of the cake and unravel the marzipan around the sides. Smooth over the sides of the cake with your hands. At the overlap, use a small, sharp knife to cut through both layers of marzipan, then carefully peel away the excess marzipan and smooth the join for a neat finish.

10 Hold the knife flush against top of the cake and trim the excess marzipan from around the edge. Trim the excess from the base with a pizza wheel, making sure not to cut too closely to the cake so as not to expose the board. Use a straight-edged smoother to smooth the marzipan and tuck in the bottom edge.

11 Hold the rounded Flexi Smoother on top of the cake and the rectangular Flexi Smoother against the side of the cake. Run the smoothers around the top edge of the cake (as if the smoothers are attached) to sharpen up the cut edge.

How TO SUGARPASTE A SHARP-EDGED ROUND CAKE

Once you have created a sharp undercoat with ganache or marzipan, you have the perfect foundation for creating a sharp-edged sugarpaste finish on your cakes. When covering the cake with sugarpaste, it is important to use smoothers to help you maintain a crisp, neat edge on your cake. I designed the Bellissimo Flexi Smoothers exactly for this purpose. With one rounded and one straight-edged smoother, you use the Flexi Smoothers together to create crisp edges for a clean finish. They are available from cake decorating shops or see page 160 for more information.

EDIBLES

Round sponge cake, layered, filled and ganached (see pages 34 to 36) or round fruit cake covered with a sharp-edged marzipan layer (see pages 39 to 40)

Sugarpaste (see table on page 43)

Icing sugar in a shaker

EQUIPMENT

Pastry brush

Kitchen roll

Non-stick rolling pin

Rolling pin rings: 5mm (¼")

Pizza wheel

Flat-edged smoother (or smedger)

Bellissimo Flexi Smoothers: small, medium or large depending on the size of the cake

Scribing tool

1 Brush the ganache or marzipan covering in all directions with a little cooled, boiled water to ensure it is covered. Brush off any excess water onto kitchen roll: the cake should be sticky to touch but not dripping wet.

 OP TIP

If the cake is covered with marzipan, brush with brandy instead of cooled, boiled water for a more traditional taste.

2 If the sugarpaste feels too firm to knead, take the required amount for the cake, break it into smaller chunks and put them on a microwaveable plate. Microwave on high power for 15 seconds then press into a piece with your thumb: the sugarpaste should feel warm and start to soften when you press it. If it is still firm, microwave for another 15 seconds. Remove from the microwave and knead well until pliable.

3 Dust the work surface with icing sugar and place the sugarpaste in the centre. Attach rolling pin rings to the ends of a rolling pin and begin to roll out. If the paste feels a little sticky, lightly dust the rolling pin and brush off any excess with your hand.

BASIC TECHNIQUES

4 Roll out the paste in one direction, turn it 45° and roll again. Keep turning and rolling out until the paste is an even 5mm (¼") thickness. Rub a smoother over the surface to even it out further. Place the rolling pin over the centre of the sugarpaste and fold one end over the pin. Lift the ends of the rolling pin and drape the sugarpaste over the cake.

5 Working quickly, smooth the paste over the top of the cake with your hands to remove any air bubbles and press the sugarpaste around the top edge to prevent it thinning. Fan out the sugarpaste down the sides of the cake to ease out any pleats, making sure you don't pull the icing down. Keep working around and down the cake until all the pleats have been eased out. Run the sides of your hands around the base of the cake.

6 Use a pizza wheel to trim the excess sugarpaste from the base of the cake. Don't cut too closely to the base or you could expose the coating underneath. Use a straight-edged smoother to press the icing firmly to the cake and tuck in the bottom edge of the sugarpaste.

7 Take the Bellissimo Flexi Smoothers and hold the straight-edged smoother to the side of the cake and the curved smoother on the top of the cake. Hold the curved smoother firmly on top of the cake with the curved edge parallel to the cake edge, then rub the rectangular smoother on the side of the cake to help create a sharp edge and polish the sides. Keep the smoother parallel to the side of the cake.

8 Once the edge starts to form, run the two smoothers together along the top edge (as if they were attached) to make it more defined. Prick any air bubbles with a scriber, wiping it clean each time so you don't mark the paste with ganache.

*T*OP TIPS

Do not sprinkle icing sugar directly on top of the sugarpaste as this will dry it out. You may need to dust more icing sugar underneath the sugarpaste, however, to stop it sticking to the work surface.

Make sure you don't push in too much on the side of the cake or you may cause the sides to slope inwards.

QUANTITIES OF SUGARPASTE FOR COVERING

The table below lists the approximate amount of sugarpaste you will need to roll out to cover the cake. You will, in fact, use about 70% of the amount suggested, but it's always best to roll out more than you need to help smooth the paste down and avoid any pleats.

Cake size	Amount of sugarpaste
10cm (4")	320g (11¼oz)
12.5cm (5")	480g (1lb 1oz)
15cm (6")	640g (1lb 6¾oz)
18cm (7")	800g (1lb 12oz)
20.5cm (8")	1.1kg (2lb 6¾oz)
23cm (9")	1.6kg (3lb 8½oz)
25.5cm (10")	1.9kg (4lb 3oz)
28cm (11")	2.4kg (5lb 6oz)
30.5cm (12")	2.7kg (6lb)

HOW TO SUGARPASTE A SHARP-EDGED SQUARE CAKE

1   Follow the steps for covering a round cake with sugarpaste up to step 4 (see opposite). Once you have draped the sugarpaste over the cake, quickly attach the paste at the corners to prevent it from tearing. Continue following the steps for covering a round cake up to step 7.

2   Hold a flat-edged smoother sideways on top of the cake and another up the side, then run the smoother firmly along the side of the cake. Repeat along each side of the cake. Hold the smoothers at the corners of the cake and press together to sharpen the angle.

3   Position the corner of a metal icing scraper on one of the corners of the cake. Using the scraper as a guide, press the straight-edged Flexi Smoother and the straight end of the curved smoother into the paste to ease it into a neat corner. Repeat for the other corners.

4   Hold the straight-edged Flexi Smoother on top and the straight end of the curved smoother on the side of the cake and run them together around the top edge (as if they were attached) to really sharpen it up. Repeat the same technique down the corners of the cake.

5   Prick any air bubbles with a scribing needle, wiping it clean each time so you don't mark the paste with ganache.

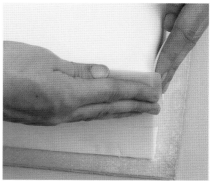

$\mathcal{H}$OW TO SUGARPASTE A CAKE DRUM (BOARD)

EDIBLES

Sugarpaste

Icing sugar in a shaker

EQUIPMENT

Cake drum (board) of required size

Pastry brush

Rolling pin rings: 3mm ($^1/_8$")

Non-stick rolling pin: large

Cake smoother

Bellissimo Flexi Smoothers: large

$\mathcal{T}$OP TIPS

The sugarpaste used to cover cakes should be as fresh as possible. However, I like to keep leftover sugarpaste for cake drums as it won't be eaten, so it doesn't matter if it has been rolled out several times.

Do not sprinkle icing sugar directly on top of the sugarpaste as this will dry it out. You may need to dust more icing sugar underneath the sugarpaste to stop it sticking to the work surface.

1 Brush the cake drum with cooled, boiled water.

2 If the sugarpaste feels too firm to knead, break the paste into smaller chunks and put them on a microwaveable plate. Microwave on high power for 15 seconds then press into a piece with your

thumb: the sugarpaste should feel warm and start to soften when you press it. If it is still firm, microwave for another 15 seconds. Remove from the microwave and knead well until pliable. If you are using leftover paste, it might be a little dry so add a sprinkle of water to make it suppler.

3 Dust the work surface with icing sugar and place the sugarpaste in the centre. Attach the rolling pin rings to the ends of the rolling pin and roll out the paste. If the paste feels a little sticky, lightly dust the rolling pin and brush off any excess with your hand.

4 Roll out the paste in one direction, turn it 45° and roll again. Keep turning and rolling out until the paste is an even 3mm ($^1/_8$") thickness and is big enough to cover the drum. Rub a smoother over the surface to even it out further. Place the rolling pin over the centre of the sugarpaste and fold one end over the pin. Lift the ends of the rolling pin and drape the sugarpaste over the drum.

5 Smooth the sugarpaste outwards from the centre with a cake smoother. Once smooth, trim the excess paste from the edge of the drum with a small, sharp knife.

6 Place the curved Flexi Smoother on top of the drum and hold the rectangular smoother at the side. Run the smoothers around the board together (as if they were attached) to neaten the trimmed edge. Allow to dry for at least 48 hours before use.

7 To finish, trim the board with a length of ribbon that is approximately 2.5cm (1") longer than the circumference of the board. Overlap the ends and secure at the back with double-sided sticky tape or a non-toxic glue stick.

ℋOW TO DOWEL A CAKE

To prevent a tiered wedding cake from collapsing, you need to support the upper tiers with cake dowels. The easiest way to do this is to scribe around a cake board the size of the tier above, then insert the dowels following the position of the numbers on a clock face. You don't need to dowel the top tier unless you are using a heavy topper.

EDIBLES

Cakes, layered, filled, ganached and sugarpasted (see pages 34 to 43)

Off-peak royal icing (see page 50)

EQUIPMENT

Cake boards the same size and shape as the upper cake tiers

Scribing tool

Large jug or bowl

Cake dowels (see table on page 46 for the amount you need)

Pencil

Clean secateurs, for sugarcraft use only

Kitchen paper

Small spirit level

Piping bag

Piping nozzle: no. 2

𝒯OP TIP

Dowels tend to come in two thicknesses: thick and extra thick. I prefer to use the thick dowels for the upper tiers and the extra thick dowels for the bottom tier.

1 Take a cake board the size of the tier directly above the cake you are dowelling. Centralise it on the top of the cake and draw around the edge with a scribing tool.

2 Fill a jug or bowl with freshly boiled water and dip a dowel into it to sterilise it, then dry with a paper towel. Remove the board from the top of the cake and insert the dowel 1.5cm (⁵/₈") inside the scribed outline at the 12 o'clock position on a clock face. Mark the dowel level with the top of the cake using a pencil, then remove the dowel and wipe off the cake crumbs.

3 Line up all the dowels you need for this tier using a ruler to ensure they are straight. Mark them all at the same height as the mark on the first dowel. Use a pair of clean secateurs, kept especially for sugarcraft use, to cut the dowels to the same height. Sterilise the dowels in the boiled water and dry with a paper towel.

4 Insert the remaining dowels into the cake at the correct points following the table overleaf. Place the cake board back on top of the cake and use a spirit level to check that the cake is still level.

5 Fill a piping bag with off-peak royal icing and a no. 2 nozzle and pipe around the dowels to seal them in. Wipe away any excess royal icing.

BASIC TECHNIQUES

DOWELLING GUIDE

Cake size	Number of dowels	Position of dowels using the numbers on a clock face
15cm (6") 18cm (7") 20.5cm (8")	4	3, 6, 9, 12
23cm (9")	5	3, 6, 9, 12 and centre
25.5cm (10") 28cm (11") 30.5cm (12")	7	2, 4, 6, 8, 10, 12 and centre

How to stack a tiered cake

EDIBLES

Cakes, sugarpasted and dowelled (see pages 41 to 45)

Small amount of royal icing (see page 50)

EQUIPMENT

Cake boards the same size as the cakes

Sugarpasted cake drum (see page 44)

Ruler

Scribing tool

Cranked palette knife

Craft knife

1 Place a cake board the same size as the base tier onto the prepared cake drum and centralise with a ruler. Mark around the edge of the board with a scribing tool, then remove. Use a palette knife to spread some royal icing within the scribed circle.

2 Run a craft knife all the way around the bottom of the largest tier between the base board and the set-up board. Slip a cranked palette knife in-between the two boards then turn it 90° to lift the cake and release it from the set-up board. Place one hand under the cake and clean any ganache off the palette knife.

3 Lift the cake with two hands and lower it onto the cake drum, using the scribed circle to help you position it in the centre. Once the cake is nearly on the drum, place the cranked palette knife beneath the cake to help lower it into its final position. Measure several points around the cake and the edge of the board to make sure it is central.

4 Repeat steps 1–3 to stack the remaining cake tiers, using a cake board the same size as the tier above each time.

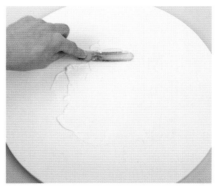

How to Assemble and Sugarpaste a Double-Barrel Cake

Double-barrel cakes are great if you want to make a feature of a cake tier, e.g. when you want to use a large monogram that wouldn't fit on a traditional tier. A double-barrel tier is also a great way to add height to a wedding cake without making it look too formal or imposing.

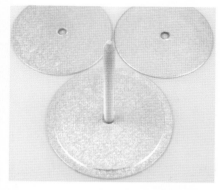

EDIBLES

2 round cake tiers (see pages 12 to 19)

Chocolate ganache (see page 28)

Sugarpaste

EQUIPMENT

5 x cake boards: 1 x cake board at least 5cm (2") larger than the cake, 2 x cake boards the same size as the cake and 2 x cake boards 2.5cm (1") smaller than the cake

1 x cake card 2.5cm (1") smaller than the cake

15mm (⁵/₈") diameter wooden dowel (see page 33)

Plastic cake dowels

Centring board (see page 32)

Electric drill with 16mm (¹⁰/₁₆") drill bit

Hot glue gun

Compass (drawing tool)

Set square

Metal rule

Non-stick rolling pins: medium and large

1 Place one of the smaller cake boards on the centring board, find the centre and mark with a pencil. Repeat for the other smaller cake board and the cake card. Use a 16mm (¹⁰/₁₆") drill bit to drill holes at the marks.

2 Use a hot glue gun to stick one of the smaller cake boards onto a larger board. Fill the hole in the board with hot glue, insert the 15mm (⁵/₈") wooden dowel and twist to secure. Scrape away any excess glue and use a set square to ensure the pole is at 90° to the board. Leave to dry.

3 Sterilise the pole and board with alcohol before use. Spread a small amount of ganache in the centre of the largest board and place the board and pole on top.

4 Layer and fill the cakes following the method on page 34 up to step 8. Assemble one of the two-tier cakes on the remaining smaller cake board and the other on the cake card.

5 Spread a 5mm (¼") layer of ganache over the top of the cake on the cake card and level with a metal rule. Allow to set.

6 Spread some ganache over the cake board with the central pole, then thread the cake with the ganache on top down the pole and lower onto the base board. Dowel the cake (see page 45).

7   Cut out a circle of baking paper that is the same size as the cake. Cut a small hole in the centre and sit it on top of the first cake. The paper prevents the next cake board from sticking to the ganache.

8   Thread the next tier down onto the pole: the pole shouldn't poke out of the top, but finish about 1.5cm (⅝") from the top. Continue to ganache the cake following the steps on page 34, using the remaining larger board for the lid. Due to the depth of the cake use a metal rule instead of a cake scraper to scrape the sides of the cake. Leave to set overnight.

9   To cover, roll out some sugarpaste into a strip that is slightly wider than the height of the cake and slightly longer than the circumference, and is 5mm (¼") thick. Place the cake on a turntable, then roll up the sugarpaste around a medium-sized rolling pin. Hold it up to the side of the cake and unroll the sugarpaste around the sides: you may need an extra pair of hands to help you turn the cake as you go. Rub over the paste with your hands and cut through the overlap at the join to create a neat edge. Rub over the join with your fingers to erase it. Trim any excess sugarpaste from the base of the cake, but don't cut too closely as it could expose the coating underneath.

10 Ease out the pleats around the top edge of the cake and cut away the excess. Rub a cake smoother over the top to flatten it. If the top of the cake will be visible, rub the surface with your fingers as the heat from your hands should help minimise the join lines. Follow the instructions on page 42 to create a sharp-edged finish.

BASIC TECHNIQUES

TRANSPORTING THE CAKE

Out of all the stages of making a wedding cake, the delivery of the cake to the venue is probably the most stressful part for a cake maker. To reduce stress and control the situation as much as I can, I deliver my cakes boxed in single tiers before assembling them at the venue. Cakes made using ganache are very heavy, often too heavy for a single person to carry once stacked.

The cakes are safely packed in boxes the same size as their set-up board. The combination of the ganached set-up board and base board, as well as the sugarpaste layer, ensures the cakes are well and truly stuck to the boards during transportation. For fruit cakes, I use non-toxic glue to stick the base board to the set-up board to ensure the cake stays in place.

If the design of the cake means it is more practical to stack the cake before applying the design, I would recommend using the 'central pole' technique on page 33.

CHECKLIST

I always make sure to take my toolbox with me when I set up cakes at a venue; it is also handy to write a checklist the day before of everything else I need to take. My toolbox includes most of the things that are listed as essential equipment on page 9, such as scissors, piping nozzles, paintbrushes, craft knives, extra dowels, posy picks, a spirit level, a cranked palette knife, pliers, a dusting brush, cake smoothers, a glue stick, glass-headed pins, double-sided tape, floral tape, a ruler, cardboard and hand wipes. The checklist will also usually include cake tiers, sugar flowers, a cake stand, royal icing, piping bags, extra sugarpaste, a tub of pre-boiled water and kitchen roll.

SETTING UP

The first thing I do, once I have unloaded everything, is to check the cake display table is level. Often this is not the case, especially in marquees, so I tend to place squares of cardboard under uneven table legs to help stabilise and level the table. Once the table is even, I position the cake stand on the table and use a ruler to make sure it is centralised, then I can go ahead with stacking the cake (see page 46).

 ROYAL ICING

Royal icing can be bought readymade or in powder form to which you just add water, such as SK Instant Mix Royal Icing.

I use an instant mix for most of the royal icing work in the book, but you will also notice on some of the projects that I have specified SK Professional Royal Icing or SK Extension Icing. These icing mixes have been especially created for certain types of royal icing work and are a great help when you want to achieve a professional finish.

I have also provided the following royal icing recipe which uses pure albumen, making it very strong and ideal for piping lace off-pieces. I use icing sugar made from sugar cane, as it is stronger than icing sugar made from sugar beet, and the additional acidity from the lemon juice or vinegar also helps to strengthen the albumen.

EDIBLES

15g (½oz) SK Pure Albumen

75ml (2½fl oz) tepid, pre-boiled water

A few drops of lemon juice or white wine vinegar

500g (1lb 1¾oz) icing sugar (made from sugar cane)

EQUIPMENT

Mixing bowls

Whisk

Sieve

Spatula

Electric stand mixer

1 Sprinkle the dried albumen onto the water and whisk. Cover and leave in the fridge for at least an hour to allow the albumen to dissolve.

2 Sieve the icing sugar into a mixing bowl. Add the lemon juice or vinegar to the albumen. Sieve the mixture onto the icing sugar.

3 Stir the mixture by hand to combine the ingredients. Using the paddle attachment on the stand mixer, mix on the slowest speed for 10–12 minutes.

4 Check the consistency of the royal icing: when you lift the up the icing with a spatula it should form peaks which bend over at the top. This is off-peak consistency which is used for most piped decoration and as a basis for run-out and rubbed-down icing. If the royal icing is too stiff, add a drop or two more water; if it's too soft, add more sieved icing sugar.

Run-out icing

This consistency is used to fill in larger areas on decorations that you are piping off the cake (off pieces).

1 Place a spoonful of off-peak consistency royal icing in a bowl.

2 Add one or two drops of cold, pre-boiled water and mix. Continue to add more water one or two drops at a time.

3 To test the consistency, draw a spoon or palette knife through the icing. The line you create should disappear within ten seconds. If it disappears before that, it is too runny and you will need to mix in more off-peak royal icing. If it takes longer, you will need to add one or two more drops of water.

Rubbed-down icing

To achieve this consistency, you need to work the icing with a palette knife to remove the air bubbles. This technique makes the icing more glossy and should be used for pressure piping and making embossers.

1 Transfer a spoonful of off-peak icing to a small non-stick board.

2 Use a palette knife to spread the icing backwards and forwards until it starts to look glossy.

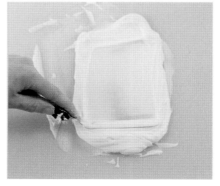

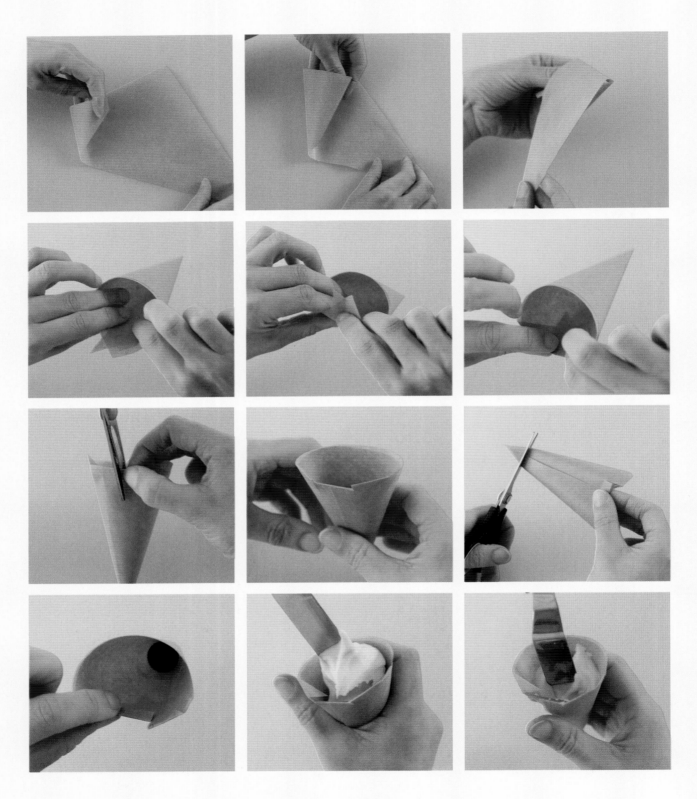

ROYAL ICING

BELLISSIMO WEDDING CAKES

How to make and fill a piping bag

1 Take a roll of greaseproof paper and measure a length that is 45.5cm (18") long. Fold over and cut along the crease with a knife.

Top Tip

I do not recommend using baking paper or baking parchment as this can make the piping bag too stiff.

2 Fold the paper over two more times and cut it into four equal rectangles that are approximately 23cm x 19cm (9" x 7½") in size.

3 Take one of the rectangles 2cm (¾") from one corner, fold it diagonally and cut. You should have two triangles with an extra 2cm (¾") strip on each: the strips help prevent the icing escaping when you are piping.

4 Lay a triangle in front of you with the longest side at the bottom. Take the blunt corner in one hand and hold the other corner with your other hand. Roll the bag into a cone with the point halfway along the bottom line.

5 Turn the bag upside down and continue to roll the bag up from the other end. The two corners should be in line with each

other and the third point to one side. Fold the points inward to create the bag.

6 Snip either side of the central seam with a pair of scissors and fold the tab over. This helps keep the bag secure.

7 Snip 2cm (¾") from the end of the bag and drop in a piping nozzle.

8 Take some prepared royal icing on the end of a palette knife and insert it into the bag until it is only half-full.

Top Tip

Filling the bag only halfway takes a lot of self-restraint, but over-filling the bag just causes the icing to ooze out of the top.

9 Flatten the end of the bag over the knife and pull the knife out of the bag.

10 Flatten and push the icing down to the bottom of the bag and remove any excess icing that has come out of the top.

11 Fold over each corner to form a point. Fold the point over then fold each 'shoulder' in. Fold over once more to finish.

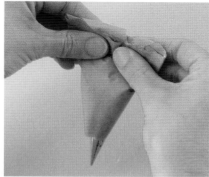

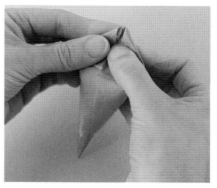

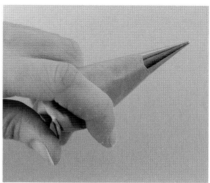

ROYAL ICING

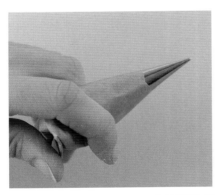

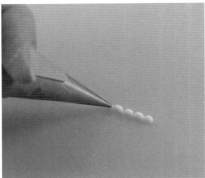

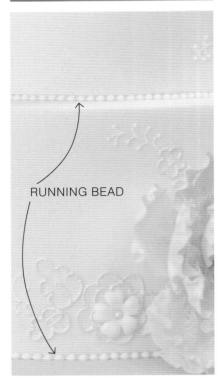

RUNNING BEAD

$\mathcal{I}$NTRODUCTION TO PIPING

If you haven't used a piping bag before, practise on a spare dummy before piping onto the final cake. Here are a few pointers which will help you achieve good results:

• Hold the piping bag between your first and middle finger and rest your thumb on top of the bag. Hold the bag in place with your fingers and use your thumb to apply the pressure on the bag to release the icing.

• If you are right-handed it is best to work left to right and if you are left-handed it is best to work right to left.

• If you are doing a lot of piping it is necessary to change the piping bag and refresh the icing every 20 minutes. Prolonged use of the same bag will cause air bubbles in the icing to expand due to the heat from your hands and will prevent the icing from flowing properly.

• When you are using several bags at one time, it is advisable to keep the ones you aren't using in a plastic food bag to prevent the icing in the nozzles from hardening over.

HOW TO PIPE A RUNNING BEAD AROUND A CAKE

To give my cakes a neat, professional-looking finish, I often pipe a simple running bead around the base of each tier. If you are piping a running bead onto stacked cakes, however, it is necessary to fill in any gaps between the tiers first.

EDIBLES

Off-peak royal icing (see page 50)

EQUIPMENT

Piping bag

Piping nozzles: nos. 2 or 3

1 Fit a piping bag with a no. 2 nozzle and half-fill with off-peak royal icing the same colour as the cake. Pipe a continuous line around the base of the tier to fill in any gaps. Tidy up with a damp paintbrush and allow to dry.

2 Fit a piping bag with a no. 2 or 3 nozzle and half-fill with royal icing in the desired colour.

3 Pipe a pearl at the base of the cake, release the pressure on the bag and pull the nozzle downwards to the right if you're right-handed or to the left if you are left-handed.

4 Apply pressure again to pipe another pearl next to the first and repeat around the base of the cake.

ROYAL ICING

MBOSSING

This simple method makes it easier to transfer an outline onto a cake, helping you achieve uniform piped designs.

EDIBLES

Rubbed-down royal icing (see page 51)

EQUIPMENT

Design template

Sheet of food-grade acrylic

Piping bag

Piping nozzles: no. 0 or 1

1 Print off or make a template of the design you wish to apply to the cake: the design needs to be reversed.

2 Lay a sheet of acrylic over the reversed design, ensuring the acrylic is parallel with the bottom line.

3 Fit a piping bag with a no. 0 or 1 nozzle and half-fill with rubbed-down royal icing. Ideally the nozzle should be one size smaller than the nozzle you will use to pipe onto the cake.

4 Pipe the design onto the acrylic, working in small sections and adjusting any wonky lines with a damp paintbrush. Leave to dry overnight.

5 Once dry, press the piped side of the embosser into the sugarpasted cake immediately after you have covered it so the paste is still soft.

6 Lightly rub over the embossed area with a Flexi Smoother to get rid of any pillowing. Leave the cake to dry overnight.

7 Once the cake is dry, the embossed lines are ready to pipe over.

OP TIP

Rubbing down the royal icing prevents it from flaking off the acrylic.

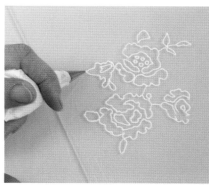

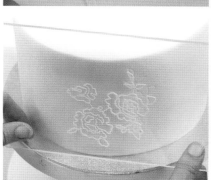

ROYAL ICING

BELLISSIMO WEDDING CAKES

$\mathscr{V}$IOLETTA

Decorated with delicate blossoms and piped flowers, this pretty, two-tier cake is beautiful outside and in. Surprise guests at a bridal shower or a small ceremony with this co-ordinating ombre sponge cake.

EDIBLES

15cm and 20.5cm (6"and 8") ombre sponge cakes coloured with SK Professional Violet Paste Food Colour (see page 21), layered, filled and ganached (see pages 34 to 36)

SK Sugarpaste (rolled fondant):
2.5kg (5lb 8¼oz) Bridal White

SK Mexican Modelling Paste (MMP): 200g (7oz) White

500g (1lb 1¾oz) SK Instant Mix Royal Icing

250g (8¾oz) SK Instant Mix Pastillage

SK Sugar Florist Paste (SFP, gum paste): 100g (3½oz) White

SK Professional Paste Food Colours: Lilac, Violet

SK Professional Dust Food Colours: Lilac, Violet

SK Quality Food Colour (QFC) Dust: Pearl

Edible pearl lustre spray (PME)

Small amount of caster sugar

Clear alcohol, e.g. gin or vodka

EQUIPMENT

Basic equipment (see pages 6 to 9)

28cm (11") round cake drum

Small daisy plunger cutter, from set of 4 (PME)

Small stephanotis cutter, from set of 3 (TT)

5-petal blossom plunger cutters: medium and large (PME)

Piping nozzles: nos. 2 x 1, 1.5 and 2 x 2

3 wooden barbecue skewers

Piece of card

Plain bead mould (Alphabet)

Satin ribbons:

   2m long x 7mm width (79" x ⁵/₁₆") purple

   1m long x 15mm width (40" x ⁵/₈") purple

Template (see page 150)

$\mathscr{D}$AISIES

1 Knead 40g (1½oz) of White MMP well, then roll it out very thinly on a non-stick board lightly dusted with cornflour. Use the small daisy cutter to cut out a few daisies at a time: you will need approximately 45 in total. Transfer the daisies to a foam pad and use a Dresden tool to shape the petals. Use a ball tool to open out the petals evenly, then spray them with edible pearl lustre spray in a well-ventilated area and leave to dry.

2 Mix a tiny amount of Lilac dust food colour with caster sugar, then colour a small amount of royal icing with a touch of Lilac dust food colour. Rub down the icing on a work surface (see page 51), fit a piping bag with a no. 1.5 nozzle and fill the bag with the icing. Pipe several small white dots on a piece of cellophane for the daisy centres. Before the icing has time to set, sprinkle the coloured sugar over the centres. Shake off and allow to dry for a few hours. Once both are dry, fix the centres into the daisies with a small amount of royal icing.

♥ ♥ ♥ SERVES 60 ♥ ♥ ♥

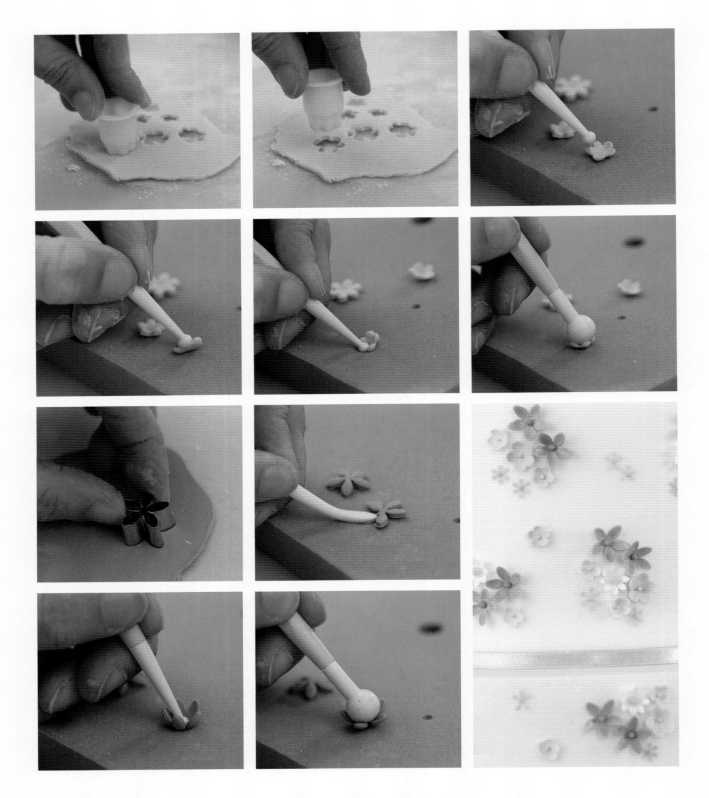

VIOLETTA

58

BLOSSOMS

3 Knead 40g (1½oz) of White MMP with a small amount of Violet paste food colour to make a pale lavender colour, and a small amount with Lilac paste food colour to make a soft lilac shade. Roll out the paste thinly and use the large and medium blossom cutters to cut out a few flowers at a time. You will need approximately 45 medium and 45 large Lilac-coloured blossoms, as well as 45 large and 40 medium Violet-coloured blossoms.

4 Place the blossoms on a foam pad, press a small ball tool into the petals to shape them, then cup the whole flower with a larger ball tool. Make some more blossoms in the same way using the Lilac-coloured paste. Spray the blossoms with edible pearl lustre spray in a well-ventilated area and allow to dry.

5 Colour small amounts of royal icing with Lilac and Violet dust food colours to make shades that match the MMP colours. Rub down the royal icing, fit two piping bags with no. 1 piping nozzles and fill them with different colours of icing. Pipe a small dot of the Violet-coloured icing in the centre of the Lilac-coloured blossoms, flattening any peaks with a damp paintbrush. Repeat with the Lilac-coloured icing and the Violet-coloured blossoms. Leave to dry.

FIVE-PETAL FLOWERS

6 Knead 40g (1½oz) of White MMP with Violet paste food colour to create a deeper violet shade. Colour another 40g (1½oz) of White MMP using Lilac paste

food colour in the same way. Roll out the MMP into a thin sheet and cut out 45 flowers of each colour using a small stephanotis cutter.

7 Place the flowers on a foam pad and shape the petals with a Dresden tool. Push a small ball tool into the flower centres to cup them, then open the petals slightly with the larger ball tool. Make some more five-petal flowers from the darker lilac-coloured paste, then spray all the flowers with edible pearl lustre spray in a well-ventilated area and allow to dry.

8 Colour small amounts of royal icing with Lilac and Violet dust food colours to make shades that match the slightly darker MMP colours. Rub down the icing, fit two piping bags with no. 2 nozzles and fill them with different colours of icing. Pipe a small dot of the contrasting colour icing into each of the five-petal flowers, flattening any peaks with a damp paintbrush. Leave to dry.

I-DO TOPPER

9 Trace the template onto a piece of card and cut it out with scissors. Place a piece of cellophane over a cake board and secure it in place with masking tape at the corners. Grease the cellophane with white vegetable fat.

10 Make up the pastillage according to the instructions on the packet. Dust a non-stick board with icing sugar and roll out the pastillage to a 6mm (¼") thickness using marzipan spacers. Grease the back of the template with white vegetable fat and position it on the paste. Use a craft knife to cut around the template. Transfer

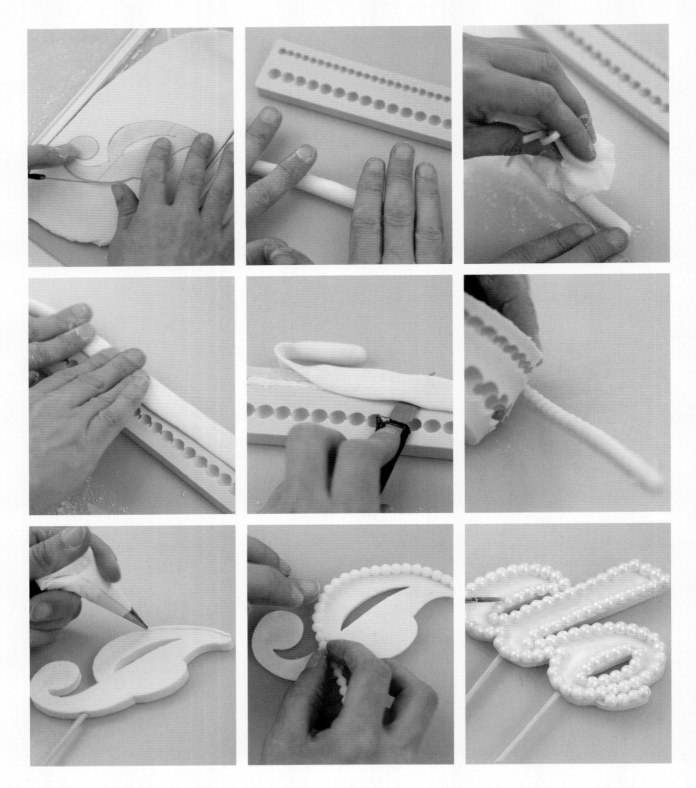

VIOLETTA

60

the pastillage to the prepared board with the template still attached. Once it is in position, remove the template and tidy the edges with a craft knife if necessary.

11 Cut the barbecue skewers at an angle, approximately 15cm (6") from the pointed end. Dip the pointed ends into some edible glue and insert each piece into the pastillage topper following the guide points on the template. Allow to dry overnight.

12 Knead a little White SFP in your hands and then roll it into a thin sausage shape. Dust with cornflour and press firmly into the smaller bead mould. Trim the excess from the back of the paste with a craft knife, then gently release the paste from the mould. You will need approximately 12 lengths of beads. Keep the lengths covered until you are ready to use them to prevent them drying out.

13 Fit a piping bag with a no. 1.5 nozzle and fill with off-peak royal icing (see page 50). Pipe around the very edge of the letters and attach the strings of beads around the pastillage topper. Use a craft knife to cut the lengths where necessary. Allow to dry.

14 Mix a little pearl lustre dust with some clear alcohol to make a metallic paint and use it to paint over the letters. Allow to dry, then dust off any excess with a soft dusting brush.

𝒜SSEMBLY

15 Cover the cakes and cake board with Bridal White sugarpaste (see pages 41 to 44) and allow to dry overnight. Dowel the 20.5cm (8") cake and stack the cakes on the board (see pages 45 to 46).

16 Fit a piping bag with a no. 1.5 nozzle and fill with off-peak royal icing. Attach clusters of lilac and violet five-petal flowers to the cake with royal icing, making sure they are evenly spaced around the cake. Start adding blossoms and daisies randomly to the clusters.

17 Pipe pale lilac and pale violet five- and six-petal flowers close to the clusters, as well as in-between the clusters. Add dots of the contrasting colour to the centres of the flowers. Stand back from the cake to check the balance of the design and fill any gaps with small blossoms to add more texture, if necessary.

18 Insert the topper into the top of the cake and secure a few flowers and blossoms around the base of the letters. Trim the cakes with 7mm (⁵/₁₆") ribbon and the board with 15mm (⁵/₈") ribbon.

Important note: Please ensure that the recipient is aware that the topper should be removed before serving as it includes wooden barbecue skewers and is made from pastillage which dries very hard.

VIOLETTA

MILIA

When I originally designed the Bellissimo Cakes logo I wanted it to look timeless and elegant so used French style scrolls to create it. This chic cake design evolved from the original monogram idea and is the perfect way to personalise a cake. The sugar peony is optional so I have separated the items you will need to make it; you may prefer to make different flowers in sugar or use fresh flowers to match the bridal bouquet.

EDIBLES

12.5cm and 23cm (5" and 9") three-layer round cakes, layered, filled and ganached (see pages 34 to 36)

18cm (7") four-layer round cake, layered, filled and ganached (see pages 34 to 36)

SK Sugarpaste: 3kg (6lb 9¾oz) Bridal White

SK Instant Mix Royal Icing: 500g (1lb 1¾oz) Tuxedo Black

Peony

SK Sugar Florist Paste (SFP, gum paste): 200g (7oz) White

SK Professional Paste Food Colours: Holly/Ivy (optional, for calyx), Rose

SK Quality Food Colour (QFC) Dust: Pearl

SK Professional Dust Food Colour: Rose

SERVES 95

EQUIPMENT

Basic equipment (see pages 6 to 9)

38cm (15") round cake drum (board)

3 sheets of food-grade acrylic

Piping nozzles: nos. 00, 0 and 1.5

Template (see page 150)

Satin ribbons:
 2m x 7mm width (79" x ¼") black
 1.5m x 35mm width (60" x 1⅜") black

Peony

3.5cm (1⅜") diameter polystyrene ball

Non-toxic craft glue

18- and 26-gauge floral wires: white

Floral tape: white

Pliers

Pasta machine (optional)

Ceramic silk veining tool

Peony petal cutters, set of 4 (CC)

5-petal cutter: 35mm (OP) (optional)

Craft knife

Deep dessertspoons and serving spoons

MBOSSERS

1 Print out the inscription for your cake in the desired font to fit the scroll frame. Trace the wording in reverse, complete with the scrolls, onto a piece of paper.

2 Position a sheet of acrylic over the design, ensuring it is lined up with the bottom line.

3 Fit a piping bag with a no. 0 nozzle and fill with rubbed-down, off-peak royal icing (see page 50). Pipe over the template, neatening any straggly lines with a damp paintbrush. Leave to dry overnight.

4 Position another piece of acrylic over the smaller scroll template and pipe over the design. Repeat with another piece of acrylic over the larger scroll. Leave both to dry overnight.

AKES

5 Cover the cakes and cake drum with Bridal White sugarpaste (see pages 41 to 44).

Emily & James

15th JUNE

EMILIA

BELLISSIMO WEDDING CAKES

6 While the sugarpaste covering is still soft, press the inscription embosser into the 18cm (7") cake. If the cake will be seen from both sides, imprint the back as well. Leave to dry.

7 Wrap a piece of greaseproof paper around the 12.5cm (5") cake to measure the circumference and cut to size. Cut the strip to 10cm (4") wide. Divide the strip into eight and position the small scroll template underneath it. Mark the central point of the scroll template onto each division line using a scribing tool.

8 Wrap the greaseproof paper around the cake again and mark the guide points around the cake using a scribing tool. Press the smaller scroll embosser into the 13cm (5") cake at the scribed points.

9 Repeat steps 7 and 8 for the 23cm (9") cake but this time divide the greaseproof paper strip into 11 and use the larger scroll template and embosser around the base of the cake. Leave all three cakes to dry.

$\mathcal{P}$IPING

10 Fit a piping bag with a no. 1.5 nozzle and fill with off-peak white royal icing.

11 Working on each tier in turn, place the cake on a tilted turntable and pipe over the embossed lines, tidying up any stray lines with a damp paintbrush. Allow to dry for at least two hours.

12 While the piping is drying, make up the Tuxedo Black royal icing. Cover the surface of the icing with cling film so that it doesn't dry out.

13 Once the first set of piping has dried, re-beat the black icing then use it to fill a piping bag fitted with a no. 00 nozzle. Pipe over the white piping, referring to the template as you work.

$\mathcal{A}$SSEMBLY

14 Dowel the cakes and stack them centrally on the covered cake drum (see pages 45 to 46).

15 Trim the cakes with the narrow black ribbon and the board with the wider ribbon (see page 44).

16 If you would like to add a sugar peony to the top of the cake, follow the instructions below then insert the stem into a posy pick and push it into the sugarpaste towards the left of the cake top.

$\mathcal{P}$EONY

FIRST STAGE

17 Cut the 18-gauge wire into thirds, then use pliers to bend a hook in the end of one of the pieces.

18 Dab a little edible glue onto the end of a hook and insert it into a 3.5cm (1³⁄₈") diameter polystyrene ball.

19 Take two 26-gauge wires and form a cross. Bend the ends of one wire over, then bend the ends of the second wire around the first to secure them together in a cross shape.

20 Place the cross over the top of the ball of paste and wrap the wires

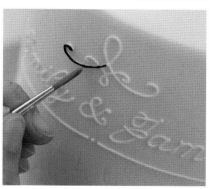

around the ball. Wrap the ends of each wire over the 18-gauge wire once to secure them in place then wrap all the ends of the wires down the 18-gauge wire.

21 Tape down the wires with white floral tape.

SECOND STAGE

22 Use a cocktail stick to add small amounts of Rose paste food colour to the SFP until you are happy with the colour. Knead thoroughly.

23 Thinly roll out some of the pale pink SFP (you can use a pasta machine for this). Cut out six small petals and slit the edges randomly with a craft knife. Cover the petals with cling film until you are ready to use them.

24 Place two of the petals onto a foam pad and roll over with a silk veining tool to add veins. Roll over the edges with the tool again until they are paper thin.

25 Brush the ball with edible glue and attach the two petals on either side, overlapping them at the top. Thin the other four petals with the silk veining tool in the same way then attach them around the first two.

THIRD STAGE

26 Thinly roll out more of the pale pink SFP and cut out five medium petals. Slit the edges and vein as before then semi-dry the petals in dessertspoons for about 10 minutes.

27 Brush edible glue halfway up the petals around the peony centre and attach the medium petals in a spiral around them, overlapping them as you work around the flower.

FOURTH STAGE

28 Cut out five large petals, trim 1cm (³/₈") off the bottom then slit and vein as before.

29 Allow the large petals to semi-dry in spoons for around 15 minutes then attach to the centre in a spiral, as before.

FIFTH STAGE

30 Cut out a further seven large petals then slit and vein as before.

31 Allow the petals to semi-dry in spoons for around 15 minutes then attach them to the flower as before.

Hang the flower upside down for 20 minutes until it holds its shape then leave to dry overnight.

32 Dust the centre with Pearl dust before moving onto the next stage.

SIXTH STAGE

33 Roll a ball of the pink SFP into a sausage. Cut a 26-gauge wire into thirds, moisten the end of one piece with edible glue and insert lengthways into the paste.

34 Use a small rolling pin to thin the paste, taking care not to roll too thinly over the wire. Cut out an extra-large petal with the wire down the centre, slit and vein as before then leave to semi-dry in a tablespoon.

35 Make four more petals in the same way and leave them to semi-dry in spoons for about 20 minutes.

36 Once the petals are firm enough to hold their shape, dust them with Rose dust, then tape around the outside of the peony flower. Dust the backs of the petals and leave to dry upside down.

SEVENTH STAGE

37 Repeat steps 33 to 36 to make another set of five extra-large petals, ensuring you position them between the previous set of petals as you tape them in place. Leave to dry upside down for three hours.

38 The calyx at the base of the flower is optional: if you would like to add one, roll out a small ball of Holly/Ivy-coloured SFP into a Mexican hat shape (see page 132). Use a 5-petal cutter to cut out the calyx and soften the edge on a foam pad with a ball tool. Push the calyx up the wire, securing to the base of the flower with edible glue. For a simpler option, tie a ribbon into a bow behind the peony to neaten the base of the flower.

EMILIA

LUCIA

Colourful candy stripes and bright bows make for a contemporary yet feminine wedding cake.
For a unique twist, why not match the colour of each sponge tier to its sugarpaste stripes?

EDIBLES

5 sponge cakes, all layered, filled and ganached (see pages 34 to 36):

    10cm (4") round, coloured with Rose

    15cm (6") round, coloured with Mint

    20.5cm (8") round, coloured with Daffodil

    25.5cm (10") round, coloured with Nasturtium

    30.5cm (12") round, coloured with Bluegrass

SK Professional Paste Food Colours: Bluegrass, Daffodil, Mint, Nasturtium, Rose

SK Sugarpaste (rolled fondant): 6kg (13lb 2oz) Bridal White

SK Sugar Florist Paste (SFP, gum paste): 1kg (2lb 3¼oz) White

Modelling paste (1kg White SFP + 1kg Bridal White Sugarpaste):

    300g (10½oz) aquamarine (White coloured with Bluegrass)

    150g (5¼oz) green (White coloured with Mint)

    250g (8¾oz) peach (White coloured with Nasturtium)

    100g (3½oz) pink (White coloured with Rose)

    1kg (2lb 3¼oz) White

    200g (7oz) yellow (White coloured with Daffodil)

Edible pearl lustre spray (PME) (optional)

EQUIPMENT

Basic equipment (see pages 6 to 9)

45.5cm (18") cake drum (board)

Pasta machine (optional)

Ribbon cutter (FMM)

Satin ribbon: 1.5m x 15mm width (60" x ⅝") white

Template (see page 151)

❤ ❤ ❤

SERVES 215

❤ ❤ ❤

CAKES

1   Colour the sponges for each tier with their respective food colours before baking. Bake following the recipe on page 12 and leave to cool.

2   Cover each cake and the cake drum with Bridal White sugarpaste and leave to dry overnight (see pages 41 to 44).

3   Knead together 1kg (2lb 3¼oz) of White SFP and 1kg (2lb 3¼oz) of Bridal White sugarpaste to make a firm modelling paste and colour as required. Wrap each piece in cling film and keep in an airtight container until ready to use.

4   Measure the circumference of the 10cm (4") cake and cut a strip of cellophane that is 15cm (6") wide and 10cm (4") longer than the circumference. Grease the strip fairly liberally with white vegetable fat.

5   Dust the work surface lightly with cornflour, knead the pink modelling paste and roll it into a thick sausage shape. Flatten down the sausage with your hands and use a rolling pin to thin out the paste even further. Feed the paste through a pasta machine until it is 2mm (1/16") thick. The strip of paste should be slightly longer than the piece of cellophane. Lay it out flat and cover

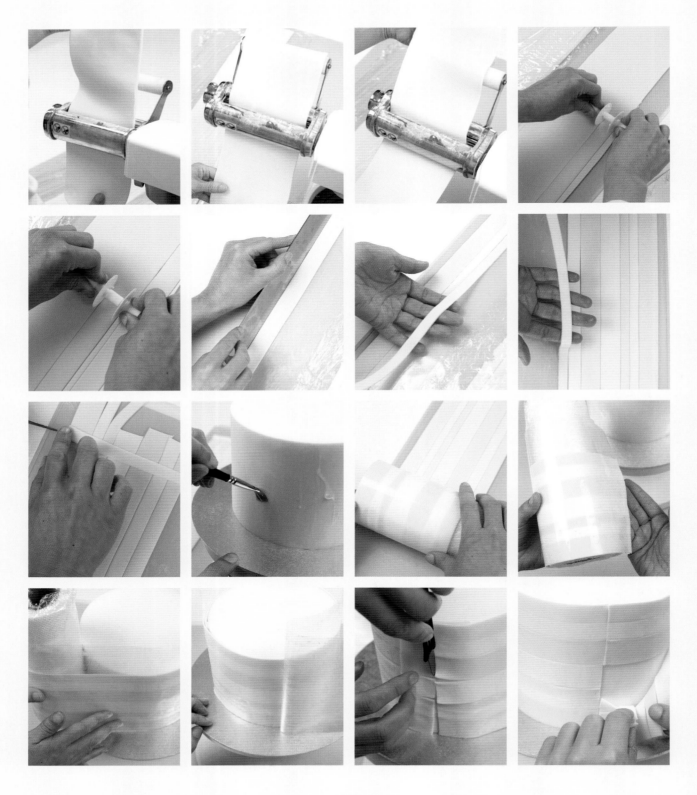

with a piece of cling film until you are ready to use it.

6 Repeat step 6 using 100g (3½oz) of white modelling paste.

7 Use the ribbon cutter to cut stripes of different widths from each length of paste, using the template as a guide.

Top Tip

You will need to press down quite firmly on the ribbon cutter. If it hasn't cut through the paste sufficiently, use a pizza wheel to finish cutting through the paste.

8 Once all the stripes have been cut, start to assemble the pattern on the greased cellophane using the template as a guide. After placing each stripe on the cellophane, use a metal rule to keep the paste straight and butt it up closely to the next stripe. Once you have finished the design, run over the paste with a cake smoother.

9 Cut two thin strips from the remaining pink modelling paste. Attach to either end of the paste to keep the stripes in place as you secure them around the cake.

10 Brush the sides of the 10cm (4") tier with edible glue. Roll up some kitchen paper to make a roll that is 6.25cm (2½") wide then wrap it in cling film: you may need to remove several sheets of paper to get the correct width.

11 Place the kitchen paper at the end of the striped pattern and carefully roll

up the pattern tightly around the roll. Secure the end of the striped paste to the cake and carefully unroll the pattern around the tier, so it slightly overlaps at the ends. Carefully peel back the cellophane. Cut through the centre of the overlapped paste with a sharp knife to make a neat join. Remove any excess sugarpaste from above and below the pattern.

12 Use a Flexi Smoother to smooth over the stripes gently then prick any air bubbles with a scribing tool. Wipe off any excess white vegetable fat with kitchen paper.

13 Repeat steps 4–12 for the remaining four tiers using the corresponding template and coloured paste.

Bows

14 Roll out 50g (1¾oz) of each colour of modelling paste. Set the ribbon cutter to 2.5cm (1") and cut a strip from the first colour of paste. Cut the strip into two pieces: a 15cm (6") length and a 6cm (2⅜") length.

15 Twist a piece of kitchen paper into a sausage to make a former and cut the paper into 5cm (2") strips.

16 Mark the centre of the 15cm (6") strip of paste and brush over the area with edible glue. Place a former either side of the centre and fold the ends over them so they meet in the middle.

17 Brush the 6cm (2⅜") strip with edible glue and place the folded bow on top of it. Fold the ends up, secure at the back and turn over for the finished bow.

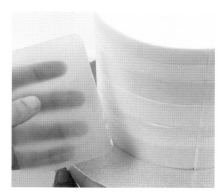

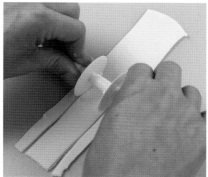

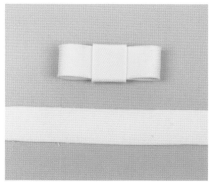

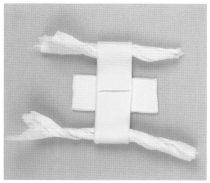

LUCIA

BELLISSIMO WEDDING CAKES

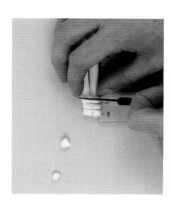
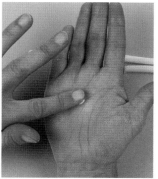
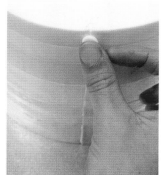
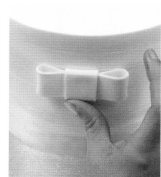

Buttons

18 Roll a small piece of coloured modelling paste into a sausage that is 8mm (5/16") in diameter and cut the paste into 5mm (¼") sections. Roll each small section into a ball and flatten slightly with a Flexi Smoother. Repeat to make approximately six buttons of each colour and 30 white buttons.

19 Attach the corresponding coloured buttons down the back of each tier, covering the joins in the stripes. Use a ruler to ensure they are in line.

Assembly

20 Dowel each cake and secure the 30.5cm (12") cake to the prepared cake board with royal icing (see pages 45 to 46). Stack the cakes, making sure the buttons line up at the back.

21 Make up some off-peak royal icing (see page 50), fit a piping bag with a no. 3 nozzle and fill with the icing. Pipe some icing onto the back of the yellow bow and secure it in the centre of the third tier on the central yellow stripe.

22 Attach the green bow to the fourth tier so that it sits slightly to the right of the centre on the widest green stripe. Position it 2.5cm (1") from the top of the cake.

23 Attach the peach bow to the second tier so that it sits slightly to the left of the yellow bow on the thickest peach stripe. It should be 2.5cm (1") from the bottom of the cake.

24 Position the pink bow on the top tier slightly further to the right than the green bow below. Attach it to the thickest pink stripe at the very top of the cake.

25 Position the aquamarine bow slightly further to the left than the peach bow above it. Attach it to the thickest aquamarine stripe at the very base of the cake.

26 Wipe off any remaining white vegetable fat with kitchen paper and allow the cakes to dry overnight.

27 Place the cake on a turntable in a well-ventilated area. Start turning the cake slowly and spray with edible pearl lustre spray, starting at the top and working your way down to get an even coverage.

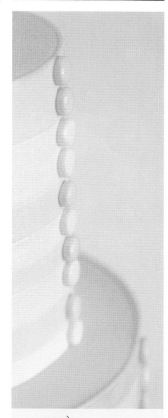

Top Tip

It is best to leave the cakes to dry overnight before spraying to help the lustre spray adhere to the surface.

 SOFIA

Inspired by the traditional royal icing techniques I learnt from Eddie Spence MBE, this sophisticated wedding cake incorporates pressure piping and hanging run-out pieces as part of a contemporary design. This graceful white cake would make an elegant centrepiece at any wedding and you can personalise the cake easily by topping it with fresh flowers to complement the bridal bouquet.

EDIBLES

3 square cakes: 15cm x 7.5cm deep, 20.5cm x 10cm deep and 25.5cm x 12.5cm deep (6" x 3", 8" x 4" and 10" x 5"), layered, filled and ganached (see pages 34 to 37)

SK Sugarpaste (rolled fondant): 3kg (6lb 9¾oz) Bridal White

1kg (2lb 3¼oz) royal icing (see page 50)

SERVES 200

EQUIPMENT

Basic equipment (see pages 6 to 9)

Square cake drums (boards): 3 x 30.5cm (12") and 5 x 40.5cm (16")

Lamp with 40-watt bulb

Piping nozzles: nos. 0, 1, 1.5, 2 and 3

3 x A5 sheets of acrylic

Square polystyrene cake separators: 10cm x 2.5cm, 15cm x 3.8cm and 20.5cm x 5cm (4" x 1", 6" x 1½" and 8" x 2")

Satin ribbons:

    50cm long x 2.5cm width (20" x 1") white

    1m long x 3.8cm width (40" x 1½") white

    1m long x 5cm width (40" x 2") white

    2m long x 7cm width (79" x 2¾") white

Templates (see pages 151 and 152)

HANGING RUN-OUT LACE PIECES

1 Cut out three 30cm (11½") squares of cellophane and fix one to each of the 30.5cm (12") cake drums, securing them at the corners with masking tape. Rub the cellophane lightly with white vegetable fat and remove any excess with kitchen roll. Place the run-out templates for each of the cakes under the cellophane on the boards.

2 Place a no. 1 nozzle in a piping bag and fill with off-peak white royal icing (see page 50). Fill two more paper piping bags with run-out consistency icing (see page 51). Pipe around the outline of the template for the 15cm (6") cake with off-peak royal icing. Snip the tip off one of the bags of run-out icing to make a hole no bigger than a no. 2 nozzle, then flood inside the outline. Place the run-out under the heat of a lamp and leave to dry. Make another four of each lace piece.

3 Repeat steps 1 and 2 using the lace templates for the 20.5cm (8") and 25.5cm (10") cakes.

SOFIA

BELLISSIMO WEDDING CAKES

I have suggested that you make five of each lace piece, although you will only need four (one for each side of the square cakes). As royal icing is very fragile once dry, I always recommend piping extra pieces in case of breakages.

4 Fit two piping bags with no. 1 and 1.5 nozzles and fill with rubbed-down royal icing (see page 51). Follow the template to pipe the floral design inside the semicircles of the run-out pieces: pipe the stem lines, leaves and half-primroses with a no. 1 nozzle, then pipe the central flower with a no. 1.5 nozzle. Leave to dry before piping the centres of the flowers.

TOP TIP

Make sure that all the piping joins up inside the lace piece or it will not be supported once you lift it into position.

5 Repeat step 4 using no. 1.5 and 2 nozzles for the 20.5cm (8") cake and no. 2 and 3 nozzles for the 25.5cm (10") cake.

6 Fit a piping bag with a no. 0 nozzle and fill with rubbed-down royal icing. Pipe a line of very small dots along the bottom of each lace piece and leave to dry. Once dry, pipe a dot in-between pairs of dots to make a triangle shape.

7 Repeat using a no. 1 nozzle for the 20.5cm (8") cake and a no. 1.5 nozzle for the 25.5cm (10") cake.

CAKES

8 Place each of the three side templates vertically under the A5 pieces of acrylic. Fit a piping bag with a no. 0 nozzle, fill with rubbed-down icing and pipe one flower design onto the acrylic. Turn the acrylic 180° to position it over the reverse flower design and pipe over it as before. Repeat for the larger templates to make three side embossers.

9 Cover the cakes with Bridal White sugarpaste using the straight-edged method (see pages 41 to 42). While the sugarpaste is still soft press the corresponding embosser into the corners on each side of the cakes, following the main image of the cake as a guide. Allow to dry overnight.

10 Fit two piping bags with no. 1 and 2 nozzles respectively and fill with rubbed-down royal icing. Pipe over the embossed markings on the 15cm (6") cake, then repeat for the 20.5cm (8") and 25.5cm (10") cakes.

11 Place the line template centrally over the top edge of the cake and use a scriber to make a mark at the top and bottom of each line. Fit a piping bag with a no. 1 nozzle and half-fill with off-peak icing. Pipe the lines down the side of the cake, starting from the top and piping down to the bottom mark. Pipe a small pearl of icing at the end of each line and flatten down any peaks with a damp paintbrush. Repeat for the 20.5cm and 25.5cm (8" and 10") cakes using the respective templates.

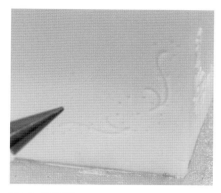

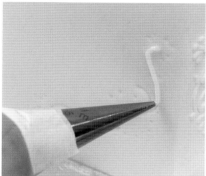

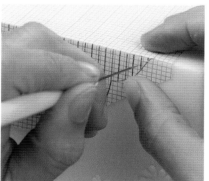

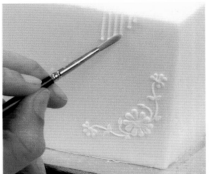

*A*SSEMBLY

12 Secure the five 40.5cm (16") square cake drums on top of each other with non-toxic glue to create a raised base. Cover the top board with a layer of Bridal White sugarpaste (see page 44) and cover the edges of the boards with the 7cm (2¾") width white ribbon.

13 Spread a small amount of royal icing over the centre of the cake drum. Position the 20.5cm (8") separator onto the board and use a ruler to make sure that it is central. Wrap the 5cm (2") width ribbon around the sides of the separator to cover them completely and secure at the back with double-sided tape. Dowel the separator (see page 45).

*T*OP TIP

Dowelling the separator prevents the weight of the cakes from crushing the polystyrene.

14 Spread a little royal icing over the first separator and position the 25.5cm (10") cake on top, making sure it is centred as before. Secure the 15cm (6") separator centrally on top of the cake, then insert a dowel into the separator and down through the cake to provide extra support, and trim to size. Insert four more dowels in the same way.

15 Stack and dowel the remaining cakes and separator as before (see pages 45 to 46).

*A*TTACHING THE LACE

16 Fit a piping bag with a no. 1.5 nozzle, fill with royal icing and pipe a line of icing along the bottom of the 15cm (6") cake. Release a 15cm (6") piece of lace from the cellophane, gently turn it over and pipe a line of icing along the top of the lace piece. Carefully centre the lace along the bottom edge of the cake: there should be 2mm–3mm (1/16"–1/8") spare on each side. Press gently onto the cake, fill any gaps with icing and tidy up any excess with a damp paintbrush. Repeat around the 15cm (6") cake.

17 Use a no. 2 nozzle to attach the appropriate lace pieces around the 20.5cm (8") cake and a no. 3 nozzle to attach the remaining lace pieces around the 25.5cm (10") cake.

18 Fill a fresh piping bag with royal icing and a no. 1.5 nozzle and use to pipe a running bead along the top of the 15cm (6") hanging pieces. Repeat using a no. 2 nozzle for the 20.5cm (8") cake and a no. 3 nozzle for the 25.5cm (10") cake.

19 Place an arrangement of fresh flowers on top of the cake to finish.

SOFIA

85

CHIARA

With its natural, rustic feel and contemporary colour scheme, this dreamy wedding cake would be perfect for an outdoor ceremony. The double-barrel tier gives the cake height and elegance and the sugar-paste decorations are simple to make.

EDIBLES

15cm and 25.5cm (6" and 10") round cakes, layered, filled and ganached (see pages 34 to 36)

20.5cm (8") round double-barrel sponge cake, layered, filled and ganached (see pages 47 to 48)

SK Sugarpaste (rolled fondant): 3kg (6lb 9¾oz) Bridal White, 250g (8¾oz) Spa Blue

SK Mexican Modelling Paste (MMP): 200g (7oz) Cream Celebration

SK Sugar Florist Paste (SFP, gum paste): 200g (7oz) Cream

500g (1lb 1¾oz) SK Professional Royal Icing, coloured pale ivory with a touch of SK Chestnut (soft beige) Professional Paste Food Colour

SK Quality Food Colour (QFC) Dust: Pearl

Clear alcohol, e.g. gin or vodka

♥ ♥ ♥ SERVES 160 ♥ ♥ ♥

EQUIPMENT

Basic equipment (see pages 6 to 9)

Thin card

Rose leaf cutters: R6, R7 (OP)

SK Great Impressions Rose Leaf Veiner: Tea Rose 5.5cm (2¼") L

Half-tube flower formers (or cardboard tubing cut in half and wrapped in cling film)

Sugar shaper (sugarcraft gun)

Satin ribbons:
    3m x 7mm width (118" x ⁵⁄₁₆") ivory
    1m x 15mm width (40" x ⁵⁄₈") ivory

Wooden dowel armature for double-barrel cake assembly (see page 33)

Pasta machine (optional)

Templates (see page 153)

CAKES

1 Knead 10g (¼oz) of Spa Blue sugarpaste into 1kg (2lb 3½oz) of Bridal White sugarpaste to achieve a pale tone of blue. Repeat for the remaining 2kg (4lb 6½oz) of Bridal White sugarpaste to make the required colour for covering the cakes and board.

2 Cover the cakes in pale blue sugarpaste using the straight-edged covering method (see pages 41 to 42), then cover the cake board in the same pale blue sugarpaste (see page 44). Leave the cakes and board to dry overnight.

WORDS

3 Enlarge the 'Love' template to 11cm (4¼") wide and the 'Cherish' template to 16.6cm (6½") wide and trace onto thin card. Cut out the word templates with a craft knife and grease the underside with white vegetable fat.

4 Roll out some Cream SFP to approximately 1mm–2mm (¹⁄₁₆") thick using a pasta machine or a rolling pin with

CHIARA

88

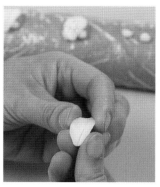

ring guides. Lay the paste onto a non-stick board and place the words on top. Press them firmly onto the paste using a smoother and use a craft knife to cut around the outlines. Turn the paste and templates over together and trim off any rough edges.

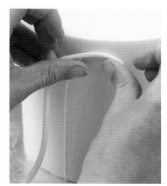

Top Tip

Do not remove any paste until you have cut all the way around the words, otherwise you may distort the lettering.

5 Paint the back of each word lightly with edible glue and position on the cakes: the word 'Love' should sit slightly to the right on the top tier and the word 'Cherish' to the left side of the base tier. Once the words are in the correct position, gently peel off the templates and allow to dry.

Leaves

6 Roll out some Cream Celebration MMP very thinly and cut out approximately 50 leaves using the smaller leaf cutter and five with the larger one. After you cut out each leaf, vein it with the rose leaf veiner then gently pinch a crease down the central line.

Drape each leaf over the tube formers and leave to dry. Roll two small balls of Cream Celebration MMP and place them underneath each leaf on either side of the crease so they dry in a natural shape.

Stems

7 Fit the sugar shaper with a 6mm (5/16") hole disc and squeeze out a length of Cream Celebration MMP. Dust a non-stick board with cornflour then use a Flexi Smoother to lengthen and slightly narrow the paste.

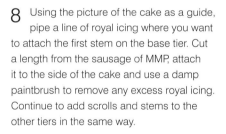

8 Using the picture of the cake as a guide, pipe a line of royal icing where you want to attach the first stem on the base tier. Cut a length from the sausage of MMP, attach it to the side of the cake and use a damp paintbrush to remove any excess royal icing. Continue to add scrolls and stems to the other tiers in the same way.

9 To attach the leaves to the stems, pipe a dot of royal icing at the base of a leaf and at the top on the underside. Attach one or two large leaves to each stem, then fill in the rest with smaller leaves.

10 Once dry, mix some Pearl lustre dust with clear alcohol and paint it over the leaves and stems.

CHIARA

BELLISSIMO WEDDING CAKES

IRDS

11 Copy the bird templates onto a thin piece of card and cut them out. Knead 50g (1¾oz) of Cream SFP with 50g (1¾oz) of Spa Blue sugarpaste to make a bright blue modelling paste. Roll the paste out to approximately 1mm–2mm (¹⁄₁₆") thick using a pasta machine or rolling pin.

12 Place the paste on a non-stick board, grease the back of the bird templates with white vegetable fat and attach firmly to the paste. Cut around the birds with a craft knife, then flip them over and trim away any rough edges. Brush over the back of the birds lightly with edible glue and attach to the centre of the middle tier, so that they are both perching on a stem. Once attached, peel off the template.

13 Using a small CelStick and the template as a guide, mark the eye, wing and tail detail on each of the birds, then soften the edges of the paste with a Dresden tool.

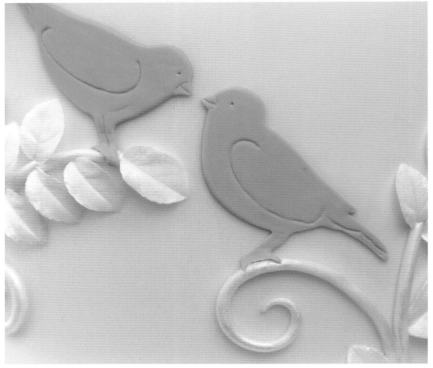

SSEMBLY

14 Dowel the base tier and stack the cakes (see pages 45 to 46), aligning the cakes so that the base tier is turned slightly to the left, the middle tier is straight on with the birds in the centre and the top tier is angled to the right.

15 Trim the base of the cakes with the 7mm (⁵⁄₁₆") width ivory ribbon, securing the ribbon at the back of each cake with a little royal icing. Trim the cake board with the 15mm (⁵⁄₈") width ivory ribbon.

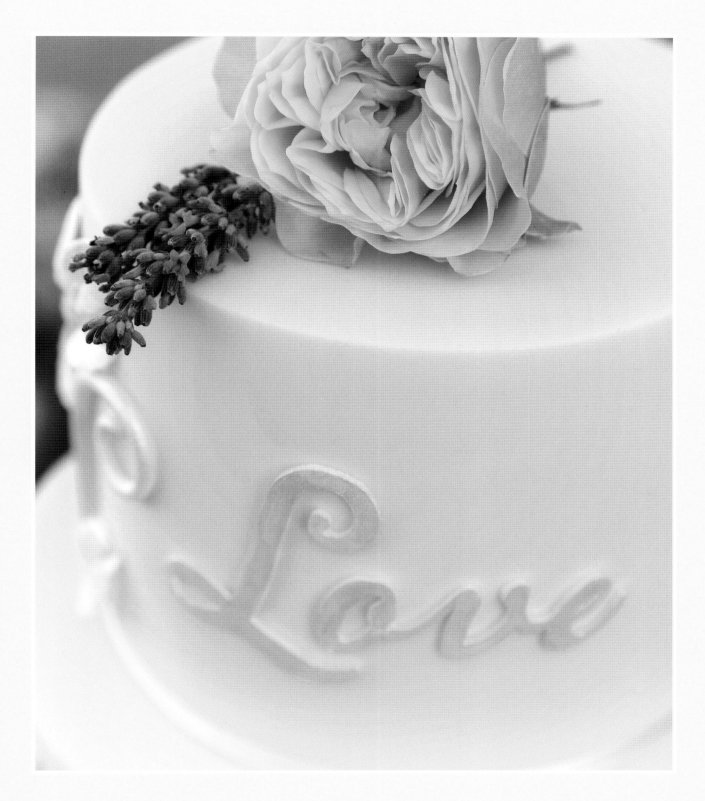

CHIARA

91

ALICIA

This imposing four-tier cake features a tumbling cascade of peonies, a real statement flower for bridal bouquets. Adorned with just a touch of sparkle, the minimalist white colour scheme gives the cake a distinctly timeless feel.

EDIBLES

12.5cm, 18cm, 23cm and 28cm (5", 7", 9" and 11") round cakes, layered, filled and ganached (see pages 34 to 36)

SK Sugarpaste (rolled fondant):
4kg (8lb 13oz) Bridal White

500g (1lb 1¾oz) SK Instant Mix Flexi-Ice

SK Sugar Florist Paste (SFP, gum paste):
1kg (2lb 3¼oz) White

SK Instant Mix Royal Icing

SK Quality Food Colour (QFC) Dust: Pearl

SK Designer Metallic Lustre Dust Food Colour: Snowflake

Clear alcohol, e.g. gin or vodka

♥ ♥ ♥
SERVES 170
♥ ♥ ♥

EQUIPMENT

Basic equipment (see pages 6 to 9)

45.5cm (18") round cake drum

2 x 35.5cm (14") round polystyrene dummies

Lace mat: Rose Mantilla (Sugarveil)

4 packets of silver diamante branches

4 packets of pearl-headed stamens

28- and 26-gauge floral wires: white

Floral tape (half-width): white

Deep dessertspoons and serving spoons

Ceramic silk veining tool

Templates (see page 153)

3 sheets of food-grade acrylic

Piping nozzles: nos. 0, 1, 1.5 and 2

Large rose petal cutters: medium and large, from set of 3 (TT)

Primrose cutters: small and medium, from set of 3 (TT)

Pliers

Satin ribbon: 1.5m x 15mm width (60" x ⅝") white

PEONY CORSAGES

You will need to make 11 peonies for the cake.

LACE PETALS

1 Make up the Flexi-Ice according to the instructions on the packet. Spread the icing thinly over the lace mat then either air-dry or leave in the oven to dry out on a low heat.

2 Once dry, carefully peel off the lace icing, roll it up in a sheet of baking paper and store in an airtight container until you need it. Repeat to make 10 more sheets of lace, as you will need one sheet per peony.

CENTRES

3 Take a diamante spray and unwind it until the three diamante decorations are all of equal height. Repeat with a second spray, then bind the two sprays together using one of the unravelled wires to make a flower centre.

ALICIA

94

4   Take 20 pearl-head stamens and place a 28-gauge wire across the centre. Fold over the stamens and use pliers to squeeze it tighter. Take one end of the wire to bind the stamens together. Make three bunches for each flower then curl the stamens over a dowel to give a natural look.

5   Tape the three stamen bunches around the diamante centre.

PETALS

6   Roll a small piece of White SFP into a ball first, then model it into a teardrop shape. Dip a 26-gauge wire into some edible glue then insert it along the length of the paste. Roll out the paste around the sides and top of the wire then cut out a petal with the medium-sized rose petal cutter so that the wire comes halfway up the length of the petal. Roll a silk veining tool over edges of the petal, flip it over and repeat on the other side. Place the petal inside a dessertspoon to give it a slightly cupped shape, then leave to semi-dry. Repeat to make five petals altogether.

7   Once all the petals are semi-dry, dust the edges with Pearl lustre dust.

8   Use the template to cut out five petals from the lace, then fold the base of each petal into a concertina. Pinch the folds together at the base of the petal, then open out the top edge. Secure each lace petal at the base of a flower paste petal with edible glue.

9   Bend the wires of the petals slightly to make them look more natural. Hold a flower centre upside down and tape the petals around the centre so they overlap slightly. Dust the backs of the petals with Pearl lustre dust and hang upside down to dry.

10 Make another 10 petals in the same way using the large cutter and tape them around the central petals in two sets of five, making sure each layer of petals is positioned in-between the last set. Allow to dry upside down.

11 Once dry, open up the petals slightly. You may need to fix the lace in place with more edible glue if it starts to fold over.

EMBOSSERS

12 Enlarge the template to the correct size and cut out two: you will need a template as it is and one in reverse. Place an acrylic sheet over the top of one of the templates. Fit a piping bag with a no. 1 nozzle, fill with rubbed-down icing and trace over the design (see page 55). Repeat for the reverse template on a second piece of acrylic. Make the bottom tier template and pipe onto another sheet of acrylic. Allow to dry overnight.

CAKES

13 Cover the cakes with Bridal White sugarpaste using the straight-edged method (see pages 41 to 42). While the paste is still soft, press the embosser into the side of each cake. For the top three tiers, allow a space of 5cm (2") between the opposite designs. For the bottom tier, allow a 15cm (6") gap between the designs and use the bottom tier template on the right-hand side. Allow to dry overnight.

14 Fit four piping bags with nos. 0, 1, 1.5 and 2 nozzles and fill each one with rubbed-down royal icing. Use the no. 1 nozzle to pipe the stems and buds. Using the no. 1.5 nozzle, pipe around the outline

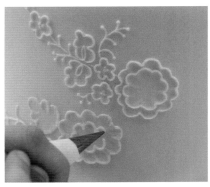

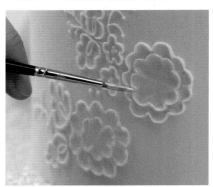

of each small flower one at a time then use a damp paintbrush to brush the icing in towards the centre of the flower. Do the same with the leaves, brushing the icing in towards the central stem. Repeat with the no. 2 nozzle for the large flowers.

15 Once dry, use a no. 0 nozzle to pipe over the outline of the flowers and leaves. Allow to dry.

16 Mix some Snowflake lustre dust with clear alcohol to make a thick paint. Paint over the outline of the flowers and leaves using a fine paintbrush.

Primroses

17 Roll out some White SFP very thinly and use the small and medium primrose cutters to cut out eight flowers in each size.

18 To shape and cup the petals, place onto a foam pad then press a small ball tool onto the top of each one and draw it downwards towards the centre of the flower. Once all the petals are cupped, flip the flower over and press the ball tool into the centre of the flower. Allow to dry.

19 Brush the primroses with Pearl dust colour. Pipe a pearl in the centre using a little rubbed-down royal icing in a piping bag with a no. 1.5 nozzle, allow to dry then paint with the thick Snowflake paint (see step 16).

20 Once all the primroses are dry, attach them to the centre of the brush embroidery flowers with a dot of royal icing.

Assembly

21 Dowel the cakes (see page 45) then stack them on top of each other. Position the bottom tier with the brush embroidery design on the left, the next tier turned slightly to the right, the next further to the right and the top tier with the design further to the right again.

22 To neaten the joins between the cakes, pipe a running bead around the base of each tier using a no. 2 nozzle and off-peak royal icing (see page 53).

23 Insert nine peonies into nine posy picks, securing the stem with a little SFP if necessary. Insert the first pick into the bottom of the base tier so that the brush embroidery design on the left just peeks out from the side of the peony. Insert another peony close to it on the right. Insert another peony above where the first two meet and another to its right.

24 Continue to insert the flower picks into the tiers, arranging the peonies between the brush embroidery decoration. For the top of the cake, tape two peonies together and insert them into a posy pick, before inserting them into the top tier.

25 To finish the cake, trim the base board with white satin ribbon.

ALICIA

97

GABRIELLA

This pretty pink cake would be perfect for a couple who want something romantic, yet a little different. The hanging scalloped lace mimics the lace edging found on many bridal gowns, giving the cake a delicate touch.

EDIBLES

15cm, 22.5cm and 30.5cm (6", 9" and 12") round cakes, layered, filled and ganached (see pages 34 to 36)

SK Sugarpaste (rolled fondant): 80g (2¾oz) Bridal Rose, 4kg (8lb 13oz) Bridal White

1.95kg (4lb 4oz) royal icing (see page 50)

SK Professional Liquid Food Colour: Rose

SK Sugar Florist Paste (SFP, gum paste): 20g (¾oz) White

EQUIPMENT

Basic equipment (see pages 6 to 9)

40.5cm (16") round cake drum

3 x round cake separators: 10cm x 2.5cm, 18cm x 3.75cm and 25.5cm x 5cm (4" x 1", 7" x 1½" and 10" x 2")

5 x round polystyrene dummies: 15cm, 2 x 23cm and 2 x 30.5cm (6", 2 x 9" and 2 x 12")

30.5cm (12") spare square cake drum

Piping nozzles: nos. 00, 0, 1, 1.5 and 2

Paintbrushes: nos. 2 and 4

Satin ribbons:

    2m x 15mm width (79" x ⅝") pale pink

    50cm x 2.5cm width (20" x 1") pale pink

    50cm x 4cm width (20" x 1½") pale pink

    50cm x 5cm width (20" x 2") pale pink

Templates (see page 154)

▼ ▼ ▼   SERVES 160   ▼ ▼ ▼

CAKES AND DRUM

1 Knead 20g (¾oz) of Bridal Rose sugarpaste into 1kg (2lb 3¼oz) of Bridal White sugarpaste to make a pale pink paste. Repeat with the remaining sugarpaste until it is all pale pink. Cover the cakes and cake drum (see pages 41 to 44) and allow to dry overnight.

LACE PIECES

2 Colour the royal icing with a very small touch of Rose liquid food colour to make a very pale pink colour.

3 Print off the lace piece template and place it onto a spare cake drum. Cut a piece of cellophane to go over the top and secure it at the corners with masking tape. Grease the cellophane lightly with white vegetable fat and remove any excess with kitchen roll.

4 Fit a piping bag with a no. 1 nozzle and fill with off-peak royal icing (see page 50). Pipe the lace pieces onto the cellophane following the template underneath. Repeat to make

GABRIELLA

approximately 120 lace pieces: it is a good idea to make a few spares to allow for breakages.

SCALLOPED LACE

5 Draw a large pentagon shape on the top of each cake dummy, positioning it so the corners of the shape reach the edge of the dummy. Use a cake leveller to slice through the dummies along the lines of each pentagon to make semicircular formers for the scalloped lace. Wrap each piece completely in cling film.

TOP TIP

Cutting through the dummies makes a lot of mess so this should be done away from the food preparation area. Vacuum up any loose polystyrene pieces before wrapping the formers in cling film.

6 Make eight copies of each scalloped lace template and tape them over each former. Cut some cellophane to the size of each former, secure over the templates and grease lightly with white vegetable fat.

7 Fit a piping bag with a no. 0 nozzle and fill with pink off-peak royal icing. Fill another piping bag with pink run-out icing (see page 51). Pipe over the outline of the first scalloped lace template for the 15cm (6") cake with the no. 0 nozzle. Snip a tiny piece off the end of the bag of run-out icing to the size of a no. 1 nozzle and flood inside the outline. Repeat with the other seven lace pieces for the 15cm (6") cake. Pipe over the templates for the 23cm (9") cake and the 30.5cm (12") cake in the same way, but using a no. 1 nozzle instead. Dry the scalloped pieces quickly by placing them

on a window sill in strong sunlight or under a desk lamp fitted with a 40-watt bulb. Once the surfaces have formed a crust, allow them to dry completely overnight.

8 Press gently on the former to release the scalloped outline and carefully place the outlines to one side. Fit one piping bag with a no. 0 nozzle and one with a no. 1 nozzle, then fill both with off-peak royal icing. Use the no. 0 nozzle to pipe the cross-hatched lines from right to left over the template, then left to right over the top of the first lines. Pipe around the cross-hatching with the no. 1 nozzle and carefully position the dried outline on top while the icing is still wet. Tidy up any royal icing that has oozed out of the sides with a damp paintbrush. Repeat for the other scalloped lace pieces and allow to dry overnight.

9 Fit another piping bag with a no. 1 nozzle and fill with off-peak royal icing. Take the smallest scalloped pieces and fill in the gap between the cellophane and the outline with royal icing, then tidy up any excess with a damp paintbrush. Repeat for the medium-sized pieces using a no. 1.5 nozzle and the largest pieces using a no. 2 nozzle.

10 Fit one piping bag with a no. 0 nozzle and another with a no. 1 nozzle, then fill them with rubbed-down royal icing (see page 51). Following the templates, pipe the stem and leaves over the cross-hatching using a no. 0 nozzle, then pipe the flowers with a no. 1 nozzle. Allow to dry, then pipe the centres of the flowers. Repeat for the medium-sized pieces using no. 1 and no. 1.5 nozzles and the larger pieces using no. 1.5 and no. 2 nozzles.

11 Gently release each scalloped lace piece by pressing your finger on the former close to the icing. Set the scalloped lace piece aside while you wipe

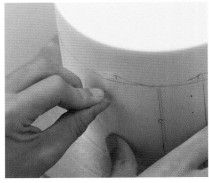

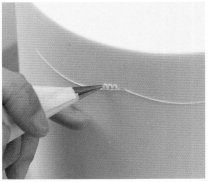

the cellophane clean of any excess royal icing and re-grease. Fit a piping bag with a no. 00 nozzle and fill with rubbed-down royal icing. Replace the lace piece on the former, then pipe a row of dots along the bottom edge. Repeat for the medium-sized pieces using a no. 0 nozzle and the largest pieces using a no. 1 nozzle.

Daisies

12 Knead 20g (¾oz) of White SFP with 20g (¾oz) of pale pink sugarpaste to make a modelling paste. Use the pink paste to make daisies in three different sizes following the instructions on page 56: you will need eight of each size.

Attaching the individual lace pieces

13 Wrap a 12.5cm (5") long piece of greaseproof paper around the 15cm (6") cake, marking the circumference and height of the cake. Fold the paper into eight equal sections and draw vertical lines at each interval. Photocopy the scallop template and enlarge or decrease the size so that it will fit into ¹/₈ of the paper, then trace the design onto each section. Cut scallops into the paper following the template then wrap the greaseproof paper around the cake. Use a scribing tool to mark the guide points and score the scalloped lines into the sugarpaste. Repeat the same process for the 23cm (9") and 30.5cm (12") cakes.

14 Fit one piping bag with a no. 0 nozzle and another with a no. 1 nozzle, then fill them both with rubbed-

down royal icing. Pipe the scalloped lines around the cake with a no. 1 nozzle. Once dry, pipe continuous M-shapes on top of the scalloped lines and pipe a bow at each of the guide points. Pipe four drop lines underneath to make the tails of the bow.

15 Find the centre of each of the scalloped lines and hold up a piece of lace to it. Using the lace as a guide, pipe two dots to secure the lace piece in place. Allow the lace to lift away from the cake slightly. Attach lace pieces either side of the first and repeat around the cake. Repeat for the 23cm (9") cake using five lace pieces per scallop and the 30.5cm (12") cake using seven lace pieces per scallop.

Assembly

16 Place the 25.5cm (10") separator on the cake drum and use a ruler to make sure it is central. Score a line around the circumference of the separator, spread a little royal icing within this circle and attach the separator to the board. Dowel the separator (see page 45) and spread more icing over the top of it. Place the 30.5cm (12") cake onto the separator then stack and dowel the 18cm (7") separator as before, ensuring you push the dowels down through the separator and into the first cake within a 15cm (6") circle. Stack and dowel the 23cm (9") cake and 10cm (4") separator within a 7.5cm (3") circle in the same way. Secure the 15cm (6") cake on top, ensuring the decoration on each tier lines up.

17 Wrap the 2.5cm (1") wide ribbon around the 10cm (4") separator to cover it and secure with double-sided tape. Repeat for the 18cm (7") and 25.5cm (10") separators using the 4cm (1½") and 5cm (2") wide ribbons respectively.

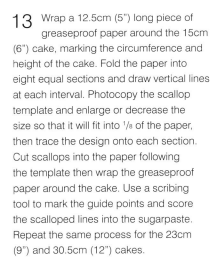

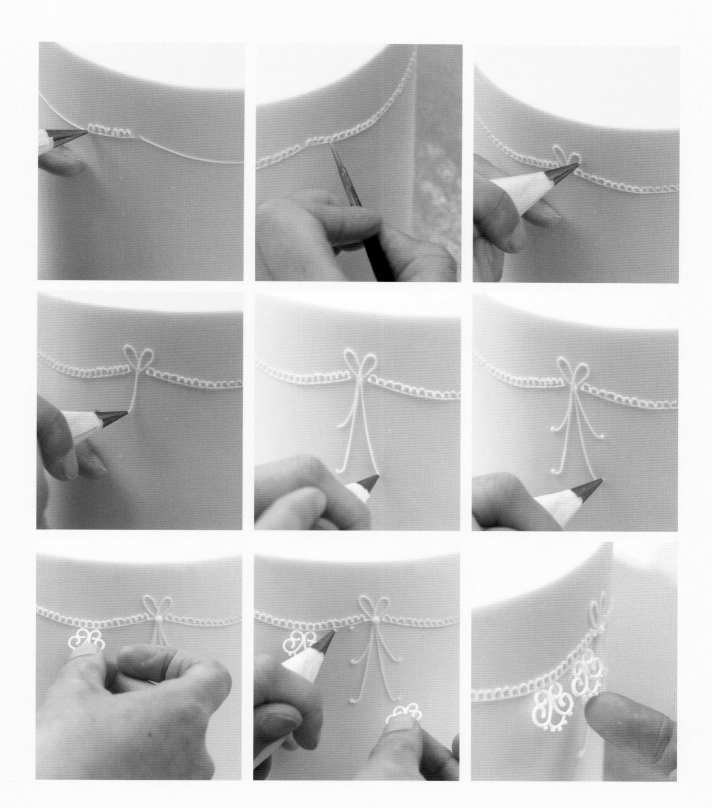

GABRIELLA

BELLISSIMO WEDDING CAKES

Attaching the Scalloped Lace

18 Fit a piping bag with a no. 1 nozzle and fill with off-peak royal icing. Following the guide points for the first set of piped scallops on the 15cm (6") cake, pipe the outline of the top of a scalloped lace piece at the bottom of the cake. Release a scalloped lace piece from its former and pipe a line of icing across the back of it. Carefully attach to the cake between the joins of the first scallops and tidy any excess royal icing with a damp paintbrush. Repeat around the rest of the cakes.

19 Once all the scalloped lace pieces are attached, pipe a running bead with a no. 1 nozzle along the top edge of each piece (see page 53). Repeat using a no. 1.5 nozzle on the 23cm (9") cake and a no. 2 nozzle on the 30.5cm (12") cake.

20 To finish, attach the daisies between the scalloped lace pieces with a dot of royal icing and secure the 15mm (⁵/₈") width ribbon around the cake drum.

GABRIELLA

$\mathcal{I}$SABELLA

I like to collect wedding and anniversary cards as they're a great indicator of current trends and a rich source of inspiration. The pretty piped scroll design was inspired by a Valentine's card and, coupled with the heart-shaped cake, is perfect for any romantic occasion.

EDIBLES

30.5cm (12") heart-shaped cake, layered, filled and ganached (see pages 34 to 36)

SK Sugarpaste (rolled fondant): 3kg (6lb 9¾oz) Antique Lace

500g (1lb 1¾oz) SK Professional Royal Icing

SK Sugar Florist Paste (SFP, gum paste): 200g (7oz) White

Edible pearl lustre spray (PME)

SERVES 90

EQUIPMENT

Basic equipment (see pages 6 to 9)

2 x 40.5cm (16") square cake drums (boards)

35cm (14") heart-shaped cake drum (board)

2 sheets of thin card

Glass-headed pins, sterilized

Piping nozzles: nos. 1 and 1.5

Blossom plunger cutters, set of 3 (PME)

Butterfly cutters: B2 and B3, from set of 4 (OP)

SK Great Impressions Hibiscus Veiner: 6cm (2³⁄₈"), from set of 3

White seed-head stamens

Satin ribbons:

    1.5m x 7mm width (60" x ¼") ivory

    2m x 2.5cm width (79" x 1") ivory

Templates (see pages 155 to 156)

$\mathcal{C}$AKE AND CAKE DRUM

1 Cover the cake with Antique Lace sugarpaste using the straight-edged method (see pages 41 to 42) and allow to dry overnight. Wrap the trimmings in cling film as they will be used later.

2 Enlarge the monogram, side design and heart design templates to the required size using a photocopier and trace them onto some greaseproof paper. Enlarge the oval template and print onto a thin piece of card, then cut out with a pair of scissors. Lay the heart design template on top of the cake and prick out the design in the sugarpaste with a scribing tool.

3 Attach the side design templates to the sides of the cake with sterilized, glass-headed pins, referring to the main picture as a guide to positioning. Again, use the scriber to mark out the designs on each side of the cake.

ISABELLA

110

Wipe the pins with alcohol to sterilize them before you insert them into the cake.

It is important to count the pins in and out to make sure that you have not left any in the cake.

4   Roll out 100g (3½oz) of Antique Lace sugarpaste to 3mm (⅛") thick and transfer the paste to a non-stick board. Grease the oval template with white vegetable fat and position on the sugarpaste. Use a craft knife to cut out the shape, then pick up the paste with the template still attached. Brush the back of the paste with edible glue and attach it centrally on top of the cake. Remove the template and rub your finger around the edge of the oval to soften it. Allow to dry overnight.

5   Fit a piping bag with a no. 1.5 nozzle and fill with off-peak royal icing (see page 50). Pipe the scrolls on the side of the cake first, following the scribed lines in the sugarpaste, and finish each scroll with a heart shape. Continue to pipe the remaining elements of the side design. Repeat for the cake-top design.

6   Knead together the remaining Antique Lace sugarpaste from the cake and cover the cake board (see page 44). Trim the board with 15mm (¾") width ivory ribbon.

LOWERS

7   Roll out a very thin sheet of White SFP onto a non-stick board. Use the different-sized plunger cutters to cut out several blossoms: you will need approximately 25 large, 45 medium and 20 small blossoms. Place each one on a foam pad and shape with a small ball tool. Press the small ball tool into the centre to cup them, then open up the petals with a large ball tool.

8   Fit a piping bag with a no. 1 nozzle and fill with rubbed-down royal icing (see page 51). Use dots of icing to fix the medium blossoms onto large blossoms and the small blossoms onto medium blossoms. Pipe a dot in the centre of each flower then allow to dry.

9   Spray all the flowers with edible pearl lustre spray in a well-ventilated area.

ℬUTTERFLIES

10   Roll out a very thin sheet of White SFP on a non-stick board then use the B3 butterfly cutter to cut out a pair of butterfly wings. Position the pair of wings together so they mirror each other. Place one wing in the centre of the 6cm (2⅜") hibiscus petal veiner and vein the paste to give it a delicate texture. Move the wing onto a foam pad and soften the edges with a ball tool. Vein the second wing in the same way, then allow them both to dry flat. Repeat to make approximately five pairs of wings from each of the B3 and B2 cutters.

11   For the bodies, roll a pea-sized amount of White SFP into a small sausage for the small butterflies and a chickpea-sized amount for the medium-sized butterflies. Cut the paste in half, taper one end to a point and round off the other end. Use a craft knife to mark a line to divide the head and body. Cut two 1cm (⅜") lengths from each end of a stamen,

then curl them slightly and insert into the head. Repeat to make another body from the other half of the paste: you will need five medium and five small bodies.

12 Fold a sheet of card into 5cm (2") wide folds to make a concertina, then open up the card and lay it on the work surface. Place a pair of wings into a V-shape between the folds and pipe a dot of icing where the wings meet. Place a body in-between the wings and use a paintbrush to remove any excess royal icing. Repeat for the remaining butterflies, making sure to match the wings with the appropriate-sized body, and allow to dry.

13 Spray all the butterflies with edible pearl lustre spray in a well-ventilated area.

ℒETTERS

14 Print off your chosen letters in the size and font you require, or copy the letters from the template onto a piece of greaseproof paper. Cut a piece of cellophane and attach it to the 15cm (6") board with small pieces of masking tape in the corners. Grease the cellophane lightly with white vegetable fat, then slide the template underneath it.

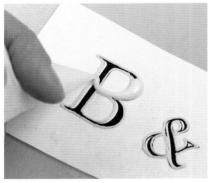

15 Fit a piping bag with a no. 1 nozzle and fill with off-peak royal icing, then fill another paper piping bag with some run-out icing. Pipe over the outline of the letters with off-peak icing, then snip off the tip of the second bag and flood inside the outlines with run-out icing (see page 51). Allow to dry.

𝒜SSEMBLY

16 Fit a piping bag with a no. 1 nozzle, fill with rubbed-down icing and pipe a row of dots around the edge of the oval plaque. Gently remove the letters from the cellophane and position centrally within the oval plaque. Use a small amount of royal icing to secure them in place.

17 Using the main picture of the cake as a guide, attach the blossoms in-between the scrolls with royal icing and secure the butterflies randomly around the cake.

18 Spread a little royal icing onto the prepared cake board and position the cake onto it centrally. Trim the cake with 7mm (¼") ribbon and secure at the back with royal icing.

ROSA

Inspired by a show-stopping wedding dress from designer Carolina Herrera, this luxurious three-tier cake is gilded with real gold leaf and crowned with golden roses, making it the perfect centrepiece for an opulent ceremony.

EDIBLES

15cm, 20.5cm and 25.5cm (6", 8" and 10") round cakes, layered, filled and ganached (see pages 34 to 36)

SK Sugarpaste (rolled fondant): 3kg (6lb 9¾oz) Vintage Ivory

SK Sugar Florist Paste (SFP, gum paste): 600g (1lb 5¼oz) Cream

30 SK Edible Gold Leaf Transfer Sheets

SK Edible Gold Leaf, book of 5 sheets

SK Designer Metallic Lustre Dust Food Colour: Light Gold

Edible glaze spray (PME)

EQUIPMENT

Basic equipment (see pages 6 to 9)

35.5cm (14") round cake drum (board)

35.5cm (14") round polystyrene dummy

Rose petal cutters, from set of 3 (TT)

SK Great Impressions Tea Rose Petal Veiner: 5.5cm (2¼") L

Rose leaf cutters:
   42mm (1½"), from set of 3 (FMM)
   Very Large, 62mm (2³⁄₈") (Framar)

SK Great Impressions Tea Rose Leaf Veiners: 7.5cm (3") VL, 4.5cm (1¾") L (from set of 4)

Floral tape (full-width and ½-width): white

18- and 26-gauge floral wires: white

Paintbrushes: small and medium

Hollow dowel, 2cm (¾") diameter (PME)

Isopropyl alcohol (IPA, dipping solution)

Satin ribbons:
   2m x 7mm width (79" x ⁵⁄₁₆") gold
   1m x 15mm width (40" x ⁵⁄₈") gold sparkly

▼ ▼ ▼   SERVES 120   ▼ ▼ ▼

CAKES AND BOARD

1   Cover all of the cakes and the cake board in Vintage Ivory sugarpaste and leave them to dry overnight (see pages 41 to 44).

MIDDLE TIER

2   Lightly brush a 12cm (4½") wide section at the top of the 20.5cm (8") cake with cooled, boiled water. Blot the side of the cake with kitchen paper so the sugarpaste is just tacky, not dripping wet. Take a gold leaf transfer sheet on its backing paper and line it up with the top edge of the cake, over the area you have dampened. Press the transfer sheet onto the cake and lightly rub the backing paper to transfer the gold leaf. Gently peel away the backing paper.

3   Dampen the area below the first gold section and position another gold leaf transfer sheet on the cake, overlapping them by approximately 5mm (¼"). Press the sheet onto the cake and rub lightly again, making sure to rub along the overlap. Continue working around the cake in small sections until you've completely covered

ROSA

116

the sides of the cake and a 5cm (2") border on top of the cake. Do not worry about any gaps at this stage. Allow to dry.

4 Once dry, fill in any gaps by first dampening the area, then cutting out a small piece of the transfer sheet and attaching it to the cake as before. Allow to dry again, then buff with a large, soft brush for a polished finish.

$\mathcal{T}$OP AND BASE TIERS

5 Dampen a paintbrush with cooled, boiled water and dab it over the bottom edge of the 15cm (6") cake. Open a book of loose gold leaf and use a craft knife to cut a sheet into small flakes, using a dry paintbrush to hold the leaf still while you cut it. Transfer the leaf pieces to the side of the cake on the dry paintbrush. Continue to cover the bottom half of the cake with small, random flakes that decrease in size and become sparser as you get further up the side of the cake.

6 Repeat for the 25.5cm (10") cake but reverse the pattern with the flakes being larger and denser at the top and around the top edge, then thinning out as you get halfway down.

7 Once all the flakes have dried in place, buff lightly with a large, soft brush.

$\mathcal{T}$OP TIP

To continue the theme at the wedding you can add tiny pieces of gold leaf to champagne.

$\mathcal{R}$OSES

You will need approximately seven full roses and six half roses, although I suggest making a few extra in case of breakages.

8 Cut a 45cm (18") length of 18-gauge floral wire in half and use fine-nosed pliers to bend a hook in one end.

9 Rub white vegetable fat into your palms and knead some Cream SFP until it is pliable. Take a small piece and seal the rest of the paste in a food-grade polythene bag to prevent it from drying out.

10 Shape the paste into a cone that is slightly smaller than the smallest rose petal cutter. Moisten the hooked end of a wire with edible glue, insert into the wide end of the cone and reshape as necessary. Insert the other end of the wire into a polystyrene dummy and leave to dry. Make 13 or more cones in the same way and leave them all to dry overnight.

11 Use a pasta machine to roll out some Cream SFP until it is almost transparent. Cut out three petals using the smallest cutter, then vein each one with the rose petal veiner and soften the edges with a ball tool. Lightly moisten one of the cones with edible glue and wrap a petal around it tightly, making sure the tip of the cone is covered.

12 Moisten ¾ of the way up the petal with edible glue and attach the next two petals around the bottom of the cone, so they are opposite each other. Tuck one petal inside the other and bend the tops of the petals outwards slightly.

13 Dust three dessertspoons with cornflour. Cut out three more petals using the smallest cutter, then vein and

ROSA

ROSA

118

soften as before. Lay a petal inside each spoon and curve the edges over the rim. Leave for five minutes until they are semi-dry.

14 Moisten the base of the rosebud with edible glue and attach the petals around the bud, making sure to overlap each petal slightly and bend the top of the petals outwards as you go. At this stage, you have a half-rose: make five more of these in the same way. Allow to dry overnight or continue to step 15 to make a full rose.

15 Dust five dessertspoons with cornflour. Using the next size of cutter, cut out and vein five petals. Lay a petal inside each spoon and curve the edges over the rim as before. Leave for 15 minutes until semi-dry.

16 Moisten the base of the half rose with edible glue, then attach one petal at a time around the base. Make sure to overlap half of each petal as you go, then tuck the last petal underneath the first to complete a full rose.

17 Hang the rose upside down on a flower rack or oven rack to firm up for approximately 30 minutes. Remove from the rack and, if necessary, adjust the petals while they are still pliable.

18 Cut out seven more petals using the same size cutter and repeat steps 15–16, leaving the rose to hang upside down for about an hour before you readjust the petals, if necessary. Allow to dry overnight.

19 Pour 100ml (3½fl oz) of IPA into a small bowl or cup. Dip a half rose

into the liquid, turn it until it is completely covered then remove. Load a large dusting brush with Light Gold lustre dust then tap off any excess. Dust gold over the back of the rose and the edges of each petal. Repeat for the rest of the half and full roses, then allow to dry.

ℒEAVES

You will need eight large leaves and 16 small leaves to make eight leaf sprays.

20 Cut eight 26-gauge wires into thirds. Roll a small piece of Cream SFP into a ball, then roll it between your hands to make a sausage shape. Dip one of the wires into some edible glue and insert it lengthways into the sausage.

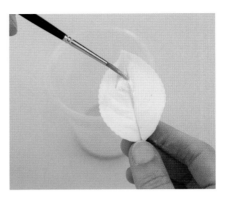

21 Use a small rolling pin to thin out the paste, taking care not to roll too firmly over the wire. Cut out a rose leaf using the 62mm (2³/₈") leaf cutter: the wire should be ²/₃ of the length of the leaf. Vein the leaf using the 7.5cm (3") rose leaf veiner, taking care not to press too firmly over the wire. Place the petal on a foam pad and soften the edges with a ball tool. Pinch the base of the leaf and twist the tip slightly to achieve a natural look. Insert the end of the wire into a polystyrene dummy and allow to dry. Repeat to make seven more leaves with the larger cutter and 16 smaller leaves with the 42mm (1½") cutter.

22 Once dry, use half-width white floral tape to tape down the length of each wire, then use the handle of a paintbrush to bend the wire gently at the base of each leaf.

23 Position two small leaves approximately 1cm (³/₈") below the base of a large leaf, then tape all three stems together. Repeat to make seven more sprays.

24 Mix some Light Gold lustre dust with clear alcohol to make a gold paint. Use a medium paintbrush to paint the

gold mixture over the leaves. Allow to dry, then spray with edible glaze spray to set the colour.

Assembling the Posy

25 Working over a piece of foam or a foam pad, tape leaf sprays onto five of the full roses. Working over the foam pad will prevent breakages in case you drop any flowers or leaves.

26 Bend an 18-gauge white wire in half and tape it in place, then measure approximately 8cm (3¹/₈") from the end of the wire and bend it to 90°. Tape one of the full-rose sprays to the end of the bent wire then tape a half rose just behind it, tucking it slightly underneath a leaf. Tape another full-rose spray and a half rose directly behind the first roses.

27 Add another full-rose spray to either end of the posy to make it crescent-shaped. Fill any gaps in the spray with half roses and leaf sprays. Insert the arrangement into a dummy whilst you work on the other arm of the spray.

28 Bend another 18-gauge wire equally into three, tape it together to make one stem then tape a full-rose spray onto it. Tape this to the bend of the stem on the larger arrangement, then tape the last full-rose spray onto the arrangement. Adjust the arrangement until you are happy with it and fill any gaps with more leaves and half-roses.

Assembling the Cake

29 Dowel and stack the three cakes (see pages 45 to 46). Push a sterilised hollow dowel into the centre of the top tier. Place a little sugarpaste in the top, then insert the flower arrangement into the paste. Trim the base of each tier with 7mm (⁵/₁₆") gold ribbon and trim the board with 15mm (⁵/₈") gold sparkly ribbon to finish.

FIORELLA

This fabulous four-tier cake is overflowing with peonies, roses, ranunculuses, tweedia, eucalyptus leaves and blossoms, making it the perfect centrepiece for a springtime ceremony. The stylised sugar flowers spilling over the tiers and vibrant candy colours contrast with the crisp, sweeping lines of the cake.

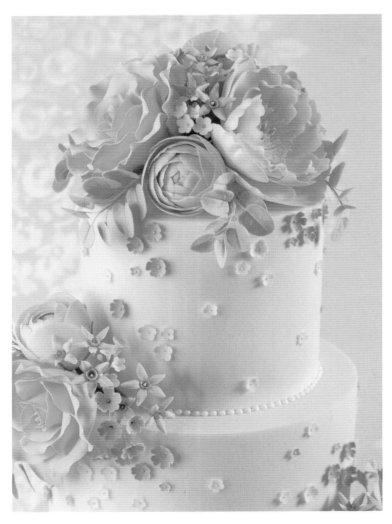

EDIBLES

Peonies

SK Sugar Florist Paste (SFP): 50g (1¾oz) Candy Green, 400g (14oz) Candy Pink, 300g (10½oz) Candy Yellow

SK Professional Dust Food Colours: Fuchsia, Leaf Green, Marigold, Rose and Sunflower

SK Designer Bridal Satin Lustre Dust Food Colour: White Satin

Ranunculuses

SK Sugar Florist Paste (SFP): 50g (1¾oz) Candy Green, 200g (7oz) Candy Pink, 200g (7oz) Candy Yellow

Roses

SK Sugar Florist Paste (SFP): 50g (1¾oz) Candy Green, 400g (14oz) Candy Peach, 170g (5¾oz) White

Tweedia

SK Sugar Florist Paste (SFP): 200g (7oz) Candy Blue, 25g (just over ¾oz) White

SK Professional Dust Food Colours: Gentian and Leaf Green

SK Designer Bridal Satin Lustre Dust Food Colour: White Satin

Eucalyptus leaves

SK Sugar Florist Paste (SFP): 200g (7oz) Candy Green

SK Designer Pastel Dust Food Colour: Soft Green

SK Designer Bridal Satin Lustre Dust Food Colour: White Satin

Blossoms

SK Sugar Florist Paste (SFP): 20g (¾oz) Candy Peach, 150g (5¼oz) Lilac, 100g (3½oz) White

SK Professional Dust Food Colours: Leaf Green and Sunflower

SK Designer Bridal Satin Dust Food Colour: White Satin

Cakes

15cm, 20.5cm, 25.5cm and 30.5cm (6", 8", 10" and 12") round cakes, layered, filled and ganached (see pages 34 to 36)

SK Sugarpaste: 5kg (11lb ¼oz) Bridal White

500g (1lb 1¾oz) SK Instant Mix Royal Icing

EQUIPMENT

Basic equipment (see pages 6 to 9)

Peonies

Peony cutters, set of 3 (or elongated rose petal cutters) (TT), for pink peony

Peony cutters, set of 4: 5cm, 5.25cm and 6.5cm (2", 2⅛" and 2½") (Culpitt), for yellow peony

Small seed-head stamens

20-, 26- and 28-gauge floral wires: white

Small pair of fine-nosed pliers

SK Great Impressions Parrot Rococo Tulip Petal Veiner: large, for pink peony

SK Great Impressions Tea Rose Petal Veiner: large, for yellow peony

CelStick

Dessertspoons

Floral tape: Nile green

Ranunculuses

Rose petal cutters, set of 4 (OP)

Rose petal cutter: 5.2cm (2⅛") (TT)

Polystyrene balls: 2cm, 2.5cm, 3cm and 4cm (¾", 1", 1⅛" and 1½")

SK Great Impressions Tea Rose Petal Veiner, 6cm (2⅜")

20- and 28-gauge floral wires: white

Small pair of fine-nosed pliers

Pasta machine (optional)

Floral tape: Nile green

Roses

18- and 26-gauge floral wires: white

Rose petal cutters: 4.5cm, 5cm, 6cm and 6.8cm (1¾", 2", 2⅜" and 2¾") (TT)

SK Great Impressions Tea Rose Petal Veiner, extra large

Pasta machine (optional)

Small pair of fine-nosed pliers

Dessertspoons and tablespoons

Large CelStick

Floral tape: Nile green

Tweedia

Stephanotis cutter set: small and medium (TT)

CelStick

Floral tape: Nile green

26-gauge floral wires: white

Small pair of fine-nosed pliers

Eucalyptus leaves

28- and 24-gauge floral wires: white

Eucalyptus leaf cutters, set of 4: small and medium (Kitbox)

SK Great Impressions Rose Leaf Veiner, 4.5cm (1¾") medium

Large CelStick

Floral tape (half-width): Nile green

Blossoms

5-petal blossom cutter set: medium and large (OP), for white blossoms

Primrose blossom cutters, set of 3: 1.5cm and 1.8cm (⅝" and ¾") (TT), for lilac blossoms

33-gauge floral wires: white

Small pair of fine-nosed pliers

Small, fine stamens

Floral tape: Nile green

Cakes

51cm (20") round cake drum

Hollow dowel rod

Piping nozzles: nos. 1, 1.5 and 3

Posy picks

Satin ribbon: 1.63m x 15mm width (64" x ⅝") white

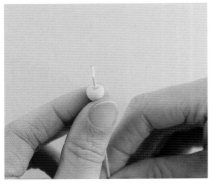

TOP TIP

I suggest making the flowers for this cake well in advance as it will take a while to make all the flowers you need. If you prefer, you could always use one or two different types of flower instead, and make them in a selection of different colours. As the flowers are stylised rather than realistic, it doesn't matter if you use a colour that you wouldn't find in nature so you can make them to match the wedding theme.

PINK PEONIES

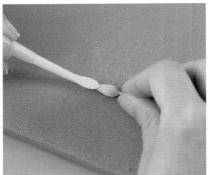

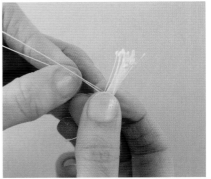

1   Cut a 20-gauge wire into thirds and bend a small hook in the end of each piece with a small pair of pliers. Roll a 6mm (5/16") ball of Candy Green SFP, insert a moistened, hooked wire into the ball and roll it into a cone shape with your fingers. Place the ball on a foam pad and flatten the end with the larger end of a Dresden tool. Twist the flattened end and leave to dry overnight. Roll five more balls and flatten them in the same way, but leave the pistils unwired. Brush the wired pistil with edible glue and attach the five unwired pistils around it. Manipulate the pistils with your fingers until you are happy with their overall appearance. Allow to dry.

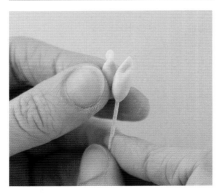

2   Mix some White Satin and Leaf Green dust food colours together and brush over the whole flower centre. Dust the ends of the pistils with Fuchsia dust food colour.

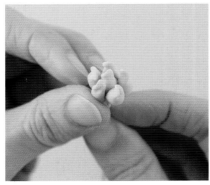

3   Cut two 28-gauge wires in half. Lay 20 small seed-head stamens over one piece of wire, positioning them 2/3 along from one end. Fold the stamens in half over the wire to form 40 ends. Twist the shorter

end of the wire around the base of the stamens to bind them together. Fan them out and curl the stamens around a CelStick. Repeat to make four more bunches.

4 Dust the stamens with Marigold dust food colour, then secure five bunches around each flower centre with Nile green floral tape and continue to tape down the wire.

5 Cut several 28-gauge wires into thirds. Roll a 2cm (¾") ball of Candy Pink SFP into a thick sausage and insert a moistened 28-gauge wire into the centre. Roll over the paste with a CelStick until the paste is thinned out, taking care not to thin too much over the wire. Cut out a small peony petal with the medium-sized cutter from the set, so the wire is approximately ²/₃ of the way up the centre of the petal. Vein the petal with a parrot tulip veiner, then place it on a foam pad. Soften and cup the petal with a ball tool, running it towards the centre of the petal. Leave to semi-dry in a dessertspoon. Make five more petals in the same way.

6 Dust ¾ of the way up the petals with a mixture of Rose, Fuchsia and White Satin dust food colours. Turn over and dust the back of each petal. Tape six petals around the flower centre using Nile green floral tape and leave to dry upside down.

7 Repeat to make six more petals with the large petal cutter, using a 26-gauge wire. Attach around the outside of the first layer of petals, positioning them in between the first six.

8 Repeat again to make six more petals with the large petal cutter and secure

around the second layer of petals. Dust the tips of all the petals with White Satin dust food colour.

9 Repeat steps 1–8 to make three more pink peonies.

Yellow Peonies

10 Follow steps 1–8 to make the flower centre in the same way as for the pink peony.

11 Roll a 2cm (¾") ball of Candy Yellow SFP and insert a 33-gauge wire into the ball. Roll out the paste thinly around the wire, then cut out a petal with the 5cm (2") peony cutter. Vein it using the large tea rose petal veiner and soften the edges with a ball tool. Draw in the edges of the petal by pulling a ball tool towards the centre. Allow to semi-dry in a dessertspoon and repeat to make six more petals.

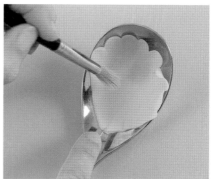

12 Dust ¾ of the way up the petals with a mixture of Sunflower and White Satin dust food colours. Tape the petals around the flower centre and allow to dry upside down.

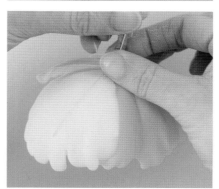

13 Make six more petals in the same way using the 5.2cm (2¹/₈") peony cutter and secure around the first layer of petals, positioning them in between the previous petals. Repeat to make six more petals with the 6.5cm (2½") cutter and secure around the flower.

14 Repeat to make another yellow peony and one yellow peony with only two layers of petals.

ℛANUNCULUSES

15 Cut a 20-gauge wire into thirds and make a hook in one end of each piece. Insert the hooked end into a 2.5cm (1") polystyrene ball.

16 Pass some Candy Green SFP through a pasta machine to roll it out into a thin sheet, then cut out five petals using the smallest petal cutter (R4). Vein each petal in a rose petal veiner and soften the edges with a ball tool. Brush the top of the polystyrene ball with edible glue then attach the petals around the very top of it, overlapping them as you go.

17 Roll out some Candy Pink SFP and cut out five petals with the R3 cutter. Vein them with a rose petal veiner and soften with a ball tool. Place a petal over a 2cm (¾") polystyrene ball to cup it, make a pleat at the bottom of each petal to fit it around the ball, then secure the fold with a little edible glue. Repeat for the remaining four petals.

18 Paint a line of edible glue around the base of the green petals and attach a cupped pink petal 5mm (¼") down from the top of the ball. Attach the remaining petals around the ball so they overlap, then tuck the final petal under the first.

19 Cut out five petals using the R2 cutter and cup over a 2.5cm (1") polystyrene ball. Attach the petals around the ranunculus, starting this second layer below the overlap in the first layer of petals.

20 Repeat to make five petals using the R1 cutter and a 3cm (1⅛") polystyrene ball, then attach below the previous layer. Twist off the excess paste from the base.

21 Make five more petals using the 5.2cm (2⅛") cutter and a 4cm (1½") ball. Attach below the previous layer and twist off the excess.

22 Cut out another five petals the same size as the previous layer, shape over a 4cm (1½") ball and pleat as before, then brush with edible glue. Shape a 28-gauge wire around a 4cm (1½") ball. Lay the wire inside the pleat and fold the paste over to seal the wire in. Trim any excess paste from the base of the petal. Repeat for the remaining petals, allow them to firm up a little then tape them around the flower. Hang the flower upside down for 30 minutes to firm up.

23 For the calyx, cut three 8cm (3⅛") strips of green floral tape then cut them in half at an angle. Stretch the tape and twist the pointed end to make individual sepals. Attach five pieces around the base of the ranunculus to form a calyx.

24 Repeat to make four more pink ranunculuses and five yellow ranunculuses using Candy Yellow SFP.

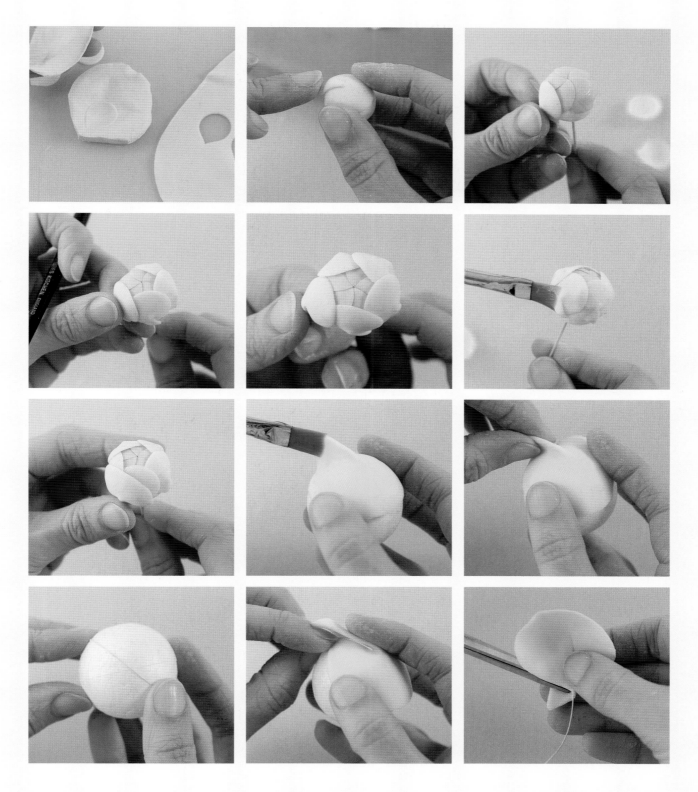

FIORELLA

129

Roses

25 Cut an 18-gauge wire into thirds and bend a small hook into the end of each piece. Roll a ball of Candy Peach SFP and insert a moistened hook into the ball. Roll the ball into a cone shape a little smaller than the smallest rose petal cutter. Allow to dry overnight.

26 Use a pasta machine to roll out some Candy Peach SFP very thinly. Cut out three petals using the smallest rose petal cutter, then vein and soften the edges of each petal. Moisten the cone with edible glue then wrap the first petal around it, ensuring that the tip is completely covered. Wrap the remaining two petals around the cone, tucking one under the other. Curve the top edges outwards with your fingers.

27 Make three more petals in the same way, then arrange them around the rosebud and curve the top edges outwards.

28 Mix 300g (10½oz) of Peach SFP with 60g (2oz) of White SFP to make a lighter colour. Roll out the paste and cut out five petals using the second smallest cutter. Vein, soften and leave to shape in dessertspoons for 10 minutes before attaching around the half-rose. Curve the tops outwards and hang upside down for 30 minutes.

29 Mix 300g (10½oz) of the lighter peach paste with another 60g (2oz) of White SFP. Roll out and cut out five more petals with the 6cm (2³⁄₈") cutter. Vein and soften as before, then leave to firm up in spoons for 10 minutes before attaching with edible glue. Hang the flower upside down for another 30 minutes.

30 Mix 250g (8¾oz) of the lighter peach paste with 50g (1¾oz) of White SFP. Roll a 3cm (1¹⁄₈") ball of paste into a thick sausage, then insert a moistened 26-gauge wire. Roll out thinly with a CelStick, taking care over the wire. Cut out a petal using the next largest cutter, making sure the wire is ²/₃ of the way up the petal. Vein, soften and leave to semi-dry in a tablespoon. Repeat to make six more. Tape the petals around the rose and hang upside down to dry.

31 Roll a 15mm (⁵⁄₈") ball of Candy Green SFP, moisten the base of the petals then thread the ball up the wire to hold the petals in place. Shape the green receptacle around the stem and remove any excess paste. Make five sepals with green tape (see page 23) and attach to the base of the rose covering the green receptacle.

32 Repeat to make three or four wired roses, then make three or four roses with unwired petals, up to step 29.

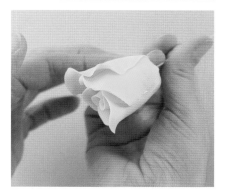

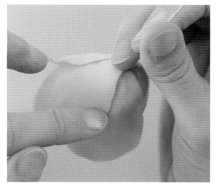

Top Tip

I gradually lighten the paste by adding more White SFP so that the outer petals are lighter than the centre, giving the flower depth.

TWEEDIA

33 Cut several white 26-gauge floral wires into thirds. Roll a small amount of White SFP onto the end of a piece of wire to make a teardrop shape.

34 Roll a 5mm (¼") ball of Candy Blue SFP and hollow out the middle with the handle of a small paintbrush. Use a craft knife to mark five vertical lines around the cone. Dampen the base of the teardrop with edible glue then pull the wire through the centre of the cone. Twist off the excess paste at the base and dust the top edge lightly with Gentian dust food colour. Allow to dry.

35 Roll a small piece of Candy Blue SFP into a thin sheet over a medium-sized hole in a grooved board. Pull away from the board and flip over so you have a Mexican hat shape. Use the medium-sized stephanotis cutter to cut a flower around the bump. Use a Dresden tool to broaden and lengthen each petal, then remove from the foam pad and hollow out the centre using the pointed end of a CelStick.

36 Moisten the base of the cone and pull the wire through the centre of the blossom, twisting off any excess paste from the base. Pinch the petals slightly to give them movement and allow to dry. Dust the petals with White Satin lustre dust.

37 Repeat steps 33–36 to make approximately 40 medium and 20 small tweedia flowers.

38 Using Nile green floral tape, tape two medium flowers and one small flower together to make a spray. Dust the white wires with Leaf Green dust food colour. Repeat to make 20 tweedia sprays.

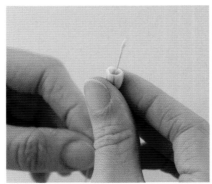

TOP TIP

As the flowers are very fragile, it is advisable to make a few spares in case of breakages.

EUCALYPTUS LEAVES

39 Cut several 28-gauge floral wires into eighths. Roll a 6mm (5/16") ball of Candy Green SFP and insert a moistened piece of wire into the centre of the ball. Roll the paste out quite thinly with a large CelStick, making sure not to press too hard over the wire. Cut out a leaf with the small eucalyptus leaf cutter, ensuring the central wire is ¾ of the way up the leaf. Place it into the top of the rose leaf veiner, press down to vein and carefully remove. Run a ball tool around the edge of the leaf, then pinch the base slightly.

40 Continue to make approximately 72 small leaves, then use the medium cutter to make approximately 72 medium-sized leaves. This will make approximately 18 stems.

41 Slightly bend the central wires of four small leaves and four medium leaves. Cut a 24-gauge wire in half, then attach two of the smallest leaves to the top of one of the pieces with half-width floral tape. Measure 1cm (3/8") down the wire and attach another pair of small leaves. Tape a pair of medium leaves 1cm (3/8") below the previous pair, then attach a final pair of medium leaves 1cm (3/8") further down the stem. Repeat to create the remaining 17 stems.

42 Dust the stems with White Satin lustre dust mixed with a little Soft Green dust food colour. Bend each of the main stems slightly to give them movement.

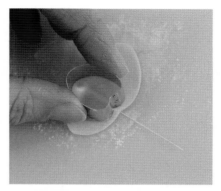

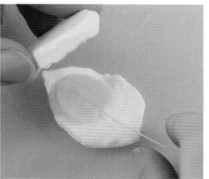

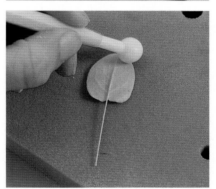

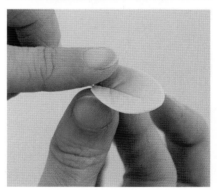

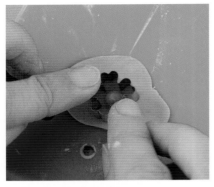

𝒲IRED BLOSSOMS

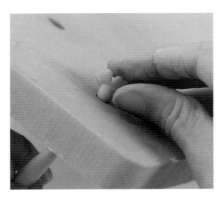

43 Roll out a 6mm (⁵⁄₁₆") ball of Lilac SFP over a large hole on a grooved board to make a Mexican hat shape. Lift up the paste and flip it over. Use the 1.8cm (1¹⁄₁₆") primrose cutter to cut out a blossom around the bump. Transfer the paste to a foam pad, positioning the bump over a hole in the pad. Soften the petals and the centre with a ball tool. Push the blossom out from the pad using the smaller end of the ball tool, rather than pulling it out and distorting the paste.

44 Cut several 33-gauge wires into thirds and make a hook in the end of each. Moisten with edible glue and thread through the centre of the blossom. Squeeze the paste around the wire to secure.

45 Cut a small stamen to 7mm (⁶⁄₁₆") long and insert it into the centre of the blossom using tweezers. Make three large blossoms and two medium-sized blossoms. Leave to dry, then dust each blossom with White Satin dust food colour and brush the stamen with Sunflower dust food colour.

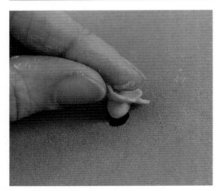

46 For each spray, tape three large and two medium blossoms together, then dust the wire with Leaf Green dust food colour. Repeat to make approximately 15–20 sprays.

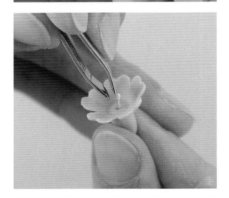

47 Repeat steps 43–46 using White SFP and the small and medium blossom cutters. Make approximately 50 larger white blossoms and 40 smaller white blossoms. You will need approximately 20 sprays.

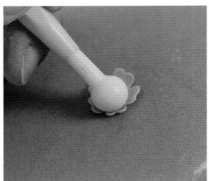

𝒰NWIRED BLOSSOMS 𝒞AKES

48 Roll out 50g (1¾oz) of White SFP, 50g (1¾oz) of Lilac SFP and 20g (¾oz) of Candy Peach SFP. Cut out several medium and large blossoms from the White SFP, several small and medium primroses from the Lilac SFP and several small and medium blossoms from the Candy Peach SFP. Shape on a foam pad and leave to dry. Brush all the dried blossoms with White Satin dust food colour.

𝒜SSEMBLY OF SPRAYS

TOP TIER ARRANGEMENT

49 Place a rose, a pink peony and a yellow peony on a piece of foam and bend the stems slightly. Hold the rose upside down, then add the peonies. Turn the flowers the right way up to check they are the same height, then turn them upside down again and tape down the stem with Nile green floral tape.

50 Take six eucalyptus stems and three ranunculus stems, then bend the wires slightly. Tape one ranunculus in between each larger flower and a eucalyptus stem on either side. Turn the arrangement the right way up before taping, just to check you are happy with the positioning. Hold the arrangement the right way up, fill any gaps with blossom and tweedia sprays and tape onto the main stem.

SIDE ARRANGEMENTS

51 For the side arrangements, tape together one large and one medium flower with a ranunculus, then add eucalyptus and blossom sprays to complete them.

52 Cover the cakes and cake board in Bridal White sugarpaste (see pages 41 to 44). Dowel and stack the cakes (see pages 45 to 46) then trim the cake board with white ribbon. Insert a hollow dowel into the top of the 15cm (6") cake and cut to size. Pipe a running bead around the base of each tier using a no. 3 nozzle (see page 54).

53 Insert the top arrangement into the hollow dowel and use a little SFP to secure it in place. Push a small ball of SFP into a posy pick then insert one of the side arrangements. Push the posy pick into the top of one of the tiers at an angle, as far from the edge as you can. Insert the remaining arrangements in the same way, spacing them evenly around the cake.

54 Fill a piping bag with a no. 1.5 piping nozzle and some off-peak royal icing (see page 50) and use it to attach the unwired blossoms around each arrangement: the blossoms should look as if they have fallen from the arrangements.

55 Colour some rubbed-down royal icing (see page 51) with Sunflower dust food colour. Fit a piping bag with a no. 1 nozzle and half-fill with the yellow icing. Pipe dots into the centre of each blossom, flattening any peaks with a damp paintbrush. Leave to dry.

𝒯OP TIP

Make sure to keep stepping back from the cake to check the positioning of the flowers.

FIORELLA

COLLEZIONE CIOCCOLATO

*Naked wedding cakes are a very popular choice, especially when the cake will be served as dessert.
This trio of chocolate cakes looks both beautiful and delicious – a layer of ganache keeps the cakes
moist whilst maintaining the understated look of a naked cake, and the piped whipped ganache
and single orchids add an elegant decorative touch.*

EDIBLES

Dark chocolate cakes layered, filled and
covered with dark chocolate ganache (see
pages 34 to 36): 15cm, 20.5cm and 25.5cm
(6", 8" and 10")

Milk chocolate cakes layered, filled and
covered with milk chocolate ganache (see
pages 34 to 36): 15cm and 20cm (6" and 8")

White chocolate cakes layered, filled and
covered with white chocolate ganache (see
pages 34 to 36): 15cm and 20cm (6" and 8")

100g (3½oz) dark chocolate ganache,
whipped for piping (see page 28)

50g (1¾oz) milk chocolate ganache,
whipped for piping (see page 28)

50g (1¾oz) white chocolate ganache,
whipped for piping (see page 28)

EQUIPMENT

Basic equipment (see pages 6 to 9)

Piping nozzle: no. 3

Templates (see page 157)

Medium posy picks

Satin ribbon: 1.2m x 7mm width (60" x
⁵⁄₁₆") purple

♥ DARK CHOCOLATE CAKE SERVES 120 │ MILK CHOCOLATE CAKE SERVES 60 │ WHITE CHOCOLATE CAKE SERVES 60 ♥

COLLEZIONE CIOCCOLATO

138

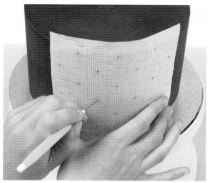

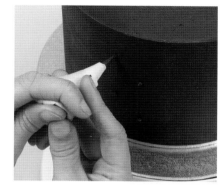

1 Copy the templates onto pieces of greaseproof paper. Use the dot template and a scribing tool to scribe the guide points onto the 15cm (6") cakes and 25.5cm (10") cake, repeating the pattern around the sides of each cake. Use the swag template to scribe the guide points for the second piped design around the sides of the 20.5cm (8") cakes.

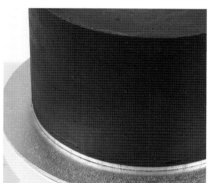

2 Fit a piping bag with a no. 3 nozzle and fill with whipped milk chocolate ganache. Following the guide dots, pipe a few dots onto the side of the 15cm (6") milk chocolate ganache cake. Flatten the peaks with a damp paintbrush before the ganache has a chance to set. Repeat around the cake, piping a few dots at a time.

3 Use the whipped milk chocolate ganache and a no. 3 nozzle to pipe the swag design around the 20.5cm (8") milk chocolate ganache cake.

4 Repeat with whipped white chocolate ganache on the white chocolate cakes and whipped dark chocolate ganache on the dark chocolate cakes.

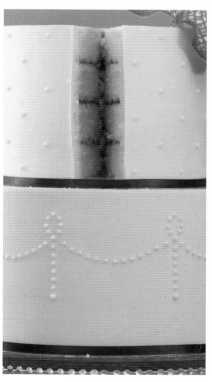

5 Dowel the 20.5cm (8") cakes and 25.5cm (10") cake, then stack the tiers using a little of the corresponding ganache to stick them in place. Finish the bottom of each tier with purple ribbon, securing at the back with a dot of ganache.

6 Place the orchids into posy picks and insert them into the cakes where desired.

CATERINA

Inspired by the wedding of the Duke and Duchess of Cambridge, this imposing five-tier cake is certainly fit for royalty. The cake incorporates a variety of piping skills, including drop-line work, extension work and pressure piping to create an intricate and impressive design.

EDIBLES

10cm, 15cm, 20.5cm, 25.5cm and 30.5cm (4", 6", 8", 10" and 12") round cakes, 9cm (3½") deep, all layered, filled and ganached (see pages 34 to 36)

SK Sugarpaste (rolled fondant): 5kg (11lb ¼oz) Vintage Ivory

SK Sugar Florist Paste (SFP, gum paste): 600g (1lb 5¼oz) Cream

1kg (2lb 3¼oz) royal icing (see page 50)

500g (1lb 1¾oz) SK Instant Mix Extension Icing

SK Designer Paste Food Colour: Cream

6 cream full roses (see pages 117 to 119)

6 cream medium rose leaves (see pages 119 to 120)

SERVES 220

EQUIPMENT

Basic equipment (see pages 6 to 9)

45.5cm and 2 x 35.5cm (18" and 2 x 14") round cake drums (boards)

12.5cm (5") square acrylic sheet

23cm round x 3.5cm deep (9" x 1³/₈") separator (or 3 x 23cm (9") cake drums stuck together)

15cm (6") round polystyrene dummy

Piping nozzles: nos. 0, 1, 1.5 and 2

33-gauge floral wire: white

Lily of the valley cutters, set of 2 (FMM)

Small daisy plunger cutter, from set of 4 (PME)

Floral tape (½-width): white

Long strip of greaseproof paper cut to 10cm (4") wide

Glass-headed pins, sterilized

Satin ribbons:

  1.5m x 15mm width (60" x ⁵/₈") ivory

  1m x 35mm width (40" x 1³/₈") ivory

Templates (see pages 158 to 159)

LILY OF THE VALLEY

1   Cut several 33-gauge wires into five equal pieces, then bend the end of each piece into a small hook.

2   Dust the largest hole in a grooved board with cornflour. Squeeze a small amount of Cream SFP into the hole and roll over the top with a large CelStick to thin out the paste. Carefully remove the paste from the hole and turn it over to make a Mexican hat shape. Position the larger lily of the valley cutter over the bump and cut out a flower shape.

3   Transfer the flower to a foam pad and soften the petals with a small ball tool. Push a medium ball tool into the centre to hollow it out. While the flower is still on the ball tool, curl up the edges of the petals with your fingers. Gently remove it from the ball tool.

4   Dip a hooked wire into some edible glue and insert the straight end of the wire into the centre of the flower and out through the base, then pull down until the hook is embedded in the flower. Curve the wire slightly and insert into a dummy to dry.

CATERINA

142

Repeat to make 42 flowers and a few extra to allow for breakages.

5 Use the medium hole in the grooved board to make 12 small flowers following the same Mexican hat method. Cut out the flowers with the smaller lily of the valley cutter, then soften the petals with the handle of a small paintbrush and hollow out with a small ball tool.

6 Roll some Cream SFP into 12 tiny balls of paste and insert a wire moistened with edible glue into each ball. Smooth the paste down onto the wire to form a bud.

7 Cut six 26-gauge wires into 20.5cm (8") lengths. Select two buds, two small flowers and eight larger flowers, then hold each stem over the template and bend the wire into the suggested shape. Repeat for the remaining flowers and buds.

8 Attach a bud to the top of a 20.5cm (8") wire with half-width floral tape, then tape another approximately 8mm ($^5/_{16}$") below and to the left-hand side. Tape a small flower 8mm ($^5/_{16}$") below to the right. Tape the next small flower 8mm ($^5/_{16}$") below again, this time in the centre. Continue to add the larger flowers in the same way, then tape down the remaining stem and curve the wire slightly.

$\mathcal{F}$LOWER ARRANGEMENT

9 Tape three lily of the valley sprays together, then tape another three further down the central stem in between the first. Bend the wires of the roses slightly at the base and tape three in front of the taller lily of the valley stems. Tape the other three in

between the first three roses underneath the shorter lily of the valley stems. Secure two leaves which curve outwards in opposite directions under each of the higher roses to fill the gaps.

$\mathcal{L}$ACE PIECES

10 Make up the royal icing then colour it pale ivory using a touch of Cream paste food colour.

$\mathcal{T}$OP TIP

Only use a very small amount of paste colouring so it does not affect the strength of the icing.

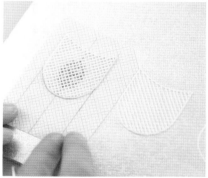

11 Position a piece of cellophane on a spare board, securing it at the corners with masking tape. Grease with white vegetable fat, then slide template A underneath the cellophane.

12 Fit a piping bag with a no. 1 nozzle and fill with off-peak royal icing (see page 50). Pipe around the outline of template A onto the cellophane, then pipe cross-hatched lines inside it. Make 26 cross-hatched panels plus a few more to allow for breakages, then allow to dry overnight.

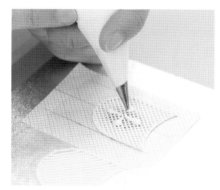

13 Rub down some royal icing (see page 51), fit a piping bag with a no. 2 nozzle and fill the bag with the icing. Following the same template, pipe a 12-petal flower in the centre of each lace panel. Pipe a dot for each of the flower centres, then allow to dry.

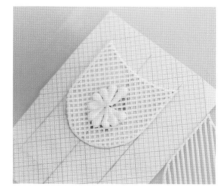

CATERINA

EMBOSSER

14 Draw out a monogram using your chosen letters and follow template B as a guide for arranging them. On the back of the paper, trace the letters in reverse using either a light box or holding the piece of paper against a window. Use the template to draw the monogram outline around the letters.

15 Fit a piping bag with a no. 0 nozzle and fill with rubbed-down royal icing. Place a piece of food-grade acrylic over the template and pipe the monogram design onto it. Allow to dry overnight.

CAKES AND CAKE DRUM

16 Cover the cakes and cake drum with Vintage Ivory sugarpaste (see pages 41 to 44). Before the icing has time to firm up, press the embosser centrally into the front of the smallest tier and gently smooth out any pillowing with a Flexi Smoother. Trim the drum with 15mm (5/8") ivory ribbon and secure with double-sided tape. Allow to dry overnight.

TOP TIP

If the cake is to be displayed in the centre of a room, you will need to emboss the monogram onto the back of the cake as well.

TOP TIER

17 Fit three piping bags with nos. 1, 1.5 and 2 nozzles respectively then fill with rubbed-down cream-coloured icing. Following the embossed design, pipe over the circle with a no. 1 nozzle. Starting at the base of the circle, pipe a small bow with a no. 2 nozzle then pipe the first third of the leaves either side of the central line. Decrease the size of the leaves slightly as you work around the circle.

TOP TIP

You may find it easier to put the cakes on a turntable when you are piping the side designs.

18 Pipe the second third of the leaves with a no. 1.5 nozzle, decreasing the size again as you work upwards. Pipe the last third of the leaves with the no. 1 nozzle, continuing to decrease the size of the leaves slightly as you reach the top. Use the no. 1.5 nozzle to pipe over the embossed monogram, squeezing the bag more firmly where the lettering thickens.

SECOND AND FOURTH TIERS

19 Make 16 small daisies from Cream SFP following the instructions on page 56 and decorate the centres with granulated sugar coloured with Cream dust food colour.

20 Take a long strip of greaseproof paper 10cm (4") wide and wrap it

around the second tier cake to measure its circumference. Cut to size and divide the length into 10 equal sections. Repeat for the fourth tier cake, dividing the paper into six equal sections. Use a photocopier to scale template C up or down to ensure it fits into a section of both cakes. Mark out each section on the cakes with a scribing tool, following the guide points on the greaseproof paper templates.

21 Fit three piping bags with nos. 1, 1.5 and 2 nozzles respectively then fill with off-peak royal icing. Use a no. 1 nozzle to pipe the first drop line: touch the nozzle just to the side of one guide point, then pull away from the cake and touch it to the side of the next point. Repeat around the cake. Use the no. 1.5 nozzle to pipe another drop line starting just underneath the first line and repeat around the cake. Pipe a third drop line underneath the second using a no. 2 nozzle and repeat around the cake.

22 Using the template as a guide, pipe a row of dots above the first drop lines. Use a no. 1 nozzle for the smallest dots at the ends, a no. 1.5 nozzle for the medium-sized dots in-between and a no. 2 nozzle for the largest central dot. Pipe a dot of royal icing at each of the guide points between the swags and fix a daisy to the cake.

THIRD TIER

23 Measure the circumference of the cake using greaseproof paper as before and divide into 12 equal sections. Scale template D up or down so it fits inside a section. Use the templates to draw scallops onto the length of greaseproof paper, then cut out the scallops. Fix the template to the centre of the cake with glass-headed pins and scribe the scallop design onto the cake. Remove the pins and the template.

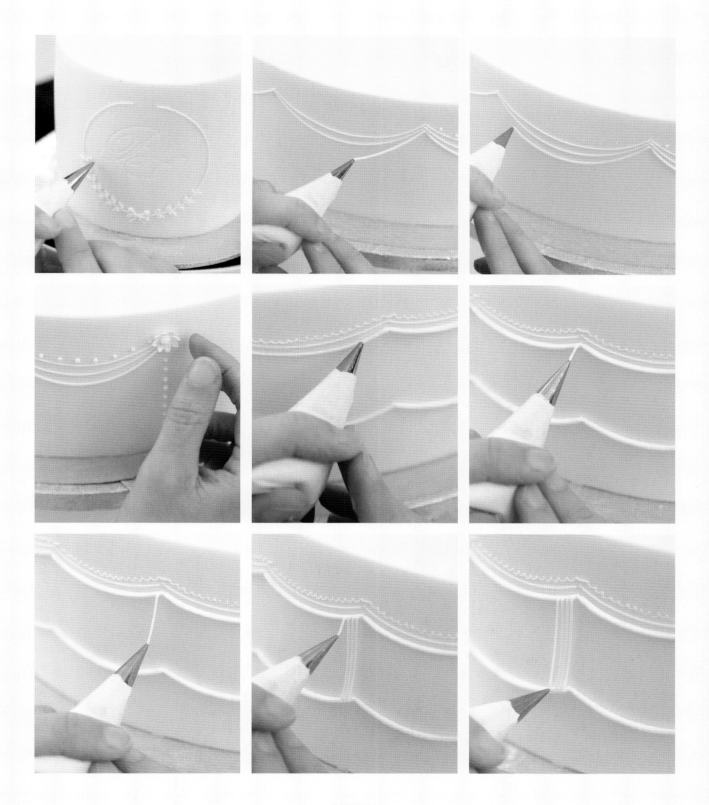

CATERINA

145

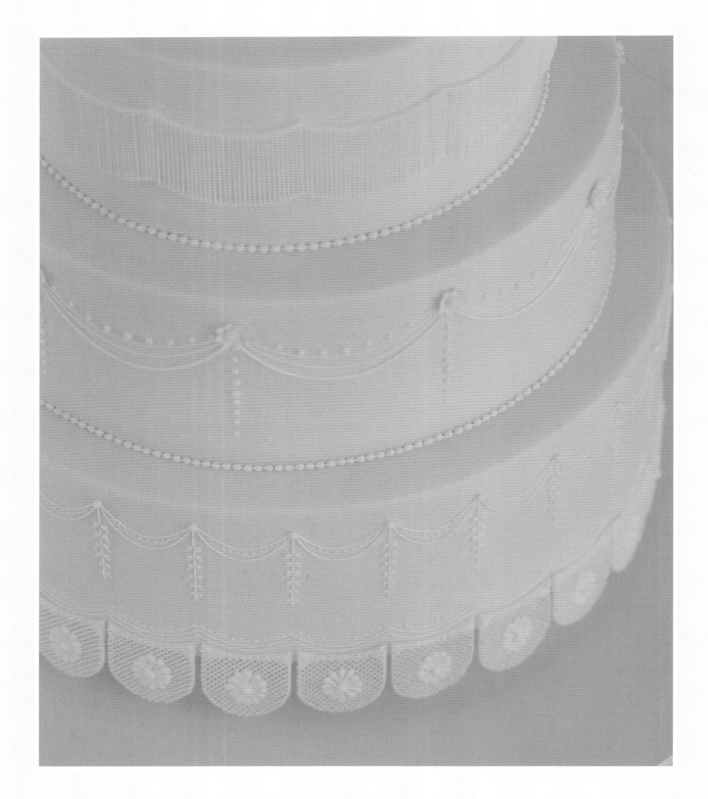

CATERINA

146

24 Fit two piping bags with a no. 0 and a no. 2 nozzle respectively then fill with off-peak royal icing. Use the no. 0 nozzle to pipe a thin scallop 3mm (¹/₈") above the top scribed line, then pipe a wiggly line above it. Use a no. 2 nozzle to pipe over the scribed lines and allow to dry. Once dry, pipe another set of lines over the first to make the bridge thicker and allow to dry again.

25 Fill a paper piping bag with some run-out consistency icing, then snip the tip off the bag. Pipe a line over the top of the bridge with run-out icing, then use a paintbrush to brush the icing into any crevices to ensure the bridge is completely smooth. Allow to dry.

26 Make up the extension icing according to the instructions on the packet. Fit a piping bag with a no. 1 nozzle and fill with the extension icing. Touch the top bridge with the tip of the nozzle, pull a line of icing away from the cake then touch it down on the bottom bridge. Repeat for the next line, leaving a gap the same thickness as the first piped line. Repeat around the cake, then leave to dry.

Top Tip

It is important not to tilt the cake because this can cause the extension lines to sag a little.

Base tier

27 Measure the circumference of the cake as for the other tiers, then divide the greaseproof paper into 26 equal sections. Scale template E up or down to fit inside one section. Use the template to mark the guide points on the paper, wrap the paper around the cake and mark out the points with a scribing tool.

28 Fit two piping bags with no. 1 and 2 nozzles respectively and fill with off-peak royal icing. Following the template as a guide, use a no. 1 nozzle to pipe two drop lines, one vertical line down from the guide points and two scallops at the bottom of each section. Use a no. 0 nozzle to pipe wavy lines between the drop lines and above the scallops.

29 Fit three more piping bags with no. 1, 1.5 and 2 nozzles and fill with rubbed-down royal icing. Use the no. 2 nozzle to pipe dots at the top of the guide marks between the swags. Flatten any peaks with a damp paintbrush.

30 Use the no. 2 nozzle to pipe two sets of leaves on either side of the vertical lines. Pipe two more sets underneath the first using a no. 1.5 nozzle. Pipe the final two sets at the bottom of the line using the no. 1 nozzle and pipe a leaf at the base of the line.

Assembly

31 Dowel the base tier, second, third and fourth tiers of the cakes and insert a hollow dowel into the centre of the top tier (see page 45). Spread a little royal icing in the centre of the prepared cake drum, secure the separator in place and dowel it in the same way as for the cakes. Secure a length of 3.5cm (1³/₈") width ivory ribbon around the separator with double-sided tape.

32 Spread royal icing over the separator, place the base tier on top and continue to stack the remaining cakes, ensuring that the piped designs are centred. Fit a piping bag with a no. 2 nozzle, fill with off-peak royal icing then pipe a running bead around the base of each cake.

33 Carefully lift a lace panel from the cellophane and turn it over. Use the no. 2 nozzle to pipe a large dot in each corner and a line of icing along the top edge. Fix to the bottom of the base tier, ensuring it sits centrally in a section. Clean up any surplus icing with a paintbrush and repeat around the cake.

34 Place a piece of SFP into the hollow dowel in the top of the cake and insert the sugar flower arrangement into it.

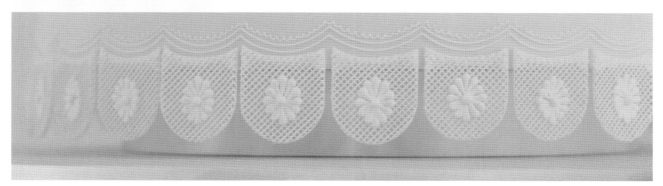

CATERINA

TEMPLATES

VIOLETTA,
pages 56–63

Dotted lines indicate guide points for skewers

EMILIA,
pages 64–71

Emily & James

15th JUNE

LUCIA,
pages 72–79
Shaded areas indicate coloured stripes

Bottom tier

1.5cm (⅝")

1cm (⅜")

2.5cm (1")

Fourth tier

2.5cm (1")

Third tier

1cm (⅜")

1.5cm (⅝")

Second tier

Top tier

2.5cm (1")

2.5cm (1")

1.5cm (⅝")

1cm (⅜")

1cm (⅜")

1.5cm (⅝")

1.5cm (⅝")

1cm (⅜")

SOFIA,
pages 80–85

15cm (6") tier
template

25.5cm (10") tier
template

20.5cm (8") tier
template

TEMPLATES

151

25.5cm (10") tier template

25.5cm (10") tier template

20.5cm (8") tier template

15cm (6") tier template

15cm (6") tier template

20.5cm (8") tier template

SOFIA,
pages 80–85

CHIARA,
pages 86-91

ALICIA,
pages 92-99

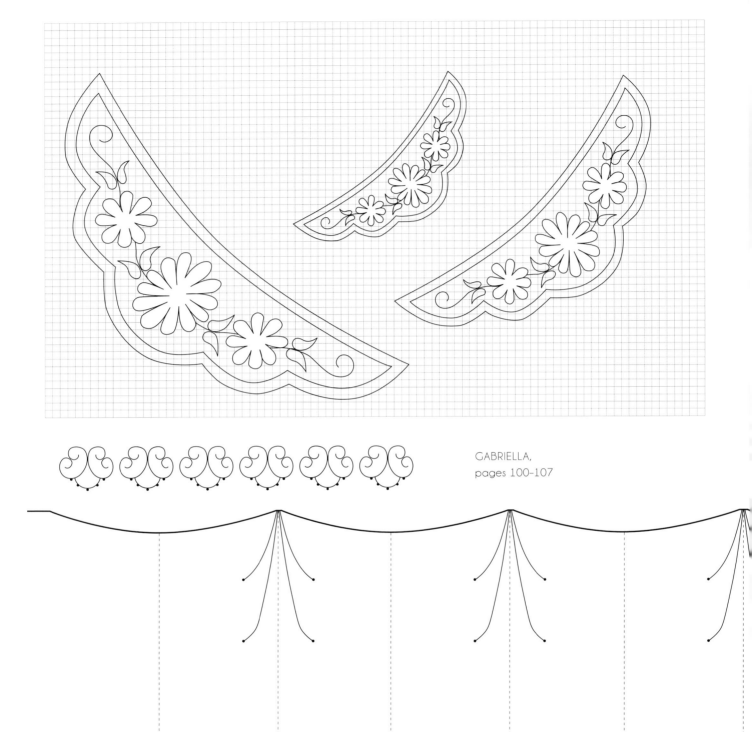

GABRIELLA,
pages 100–107

ISABELLA,
pages 108–113

Heart cake-top
template is half of the
actual size. Enlarge
the template to 200%
for the correct size.

ISABELLA,
pages 108–113

Cake side templates

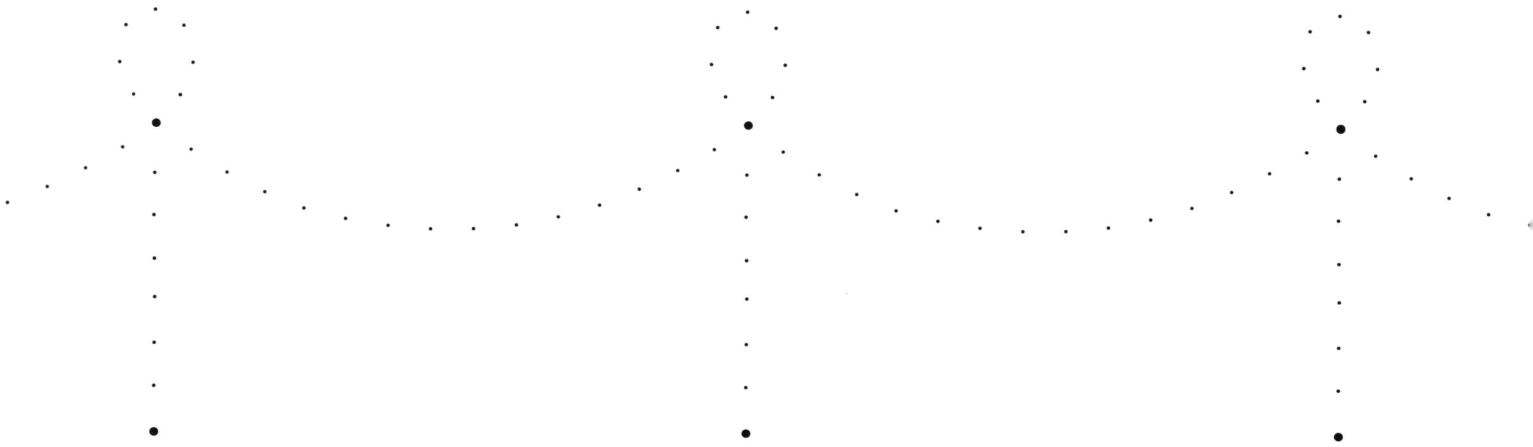

COLLEZIONE CIOCCOLATO,
pages 136-139

20.5cm (8") tier template

Bottom of tier

15cm (6") tier and 25.5cm (10") tier template

Bottom of tier

CATERINA,
pages 140-149

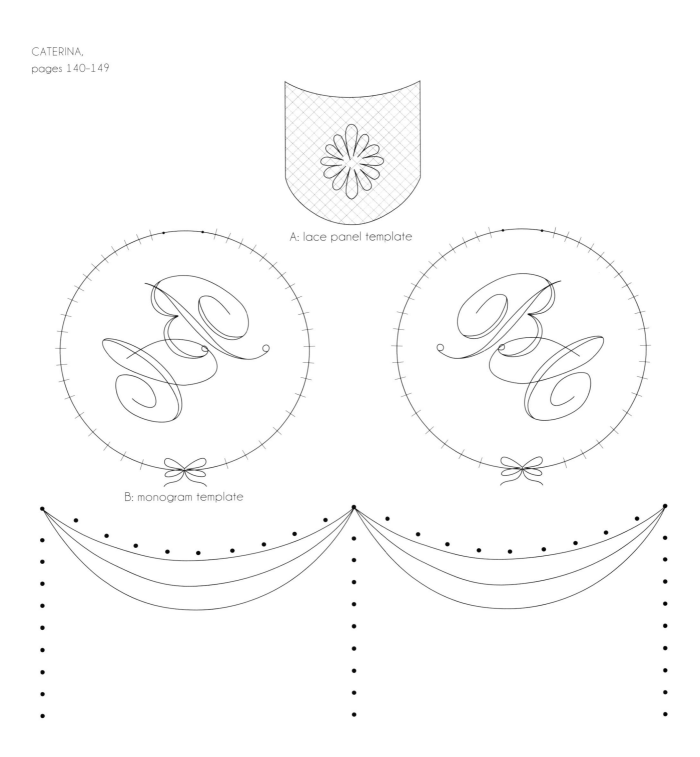

A: lace panel template

B: monogram template

Bottom of tier

C: 15cm (6") tier and 25.5cm (10") tier template

D: 20.5cm (8") tier template

E: 30.5cm (12") tier template

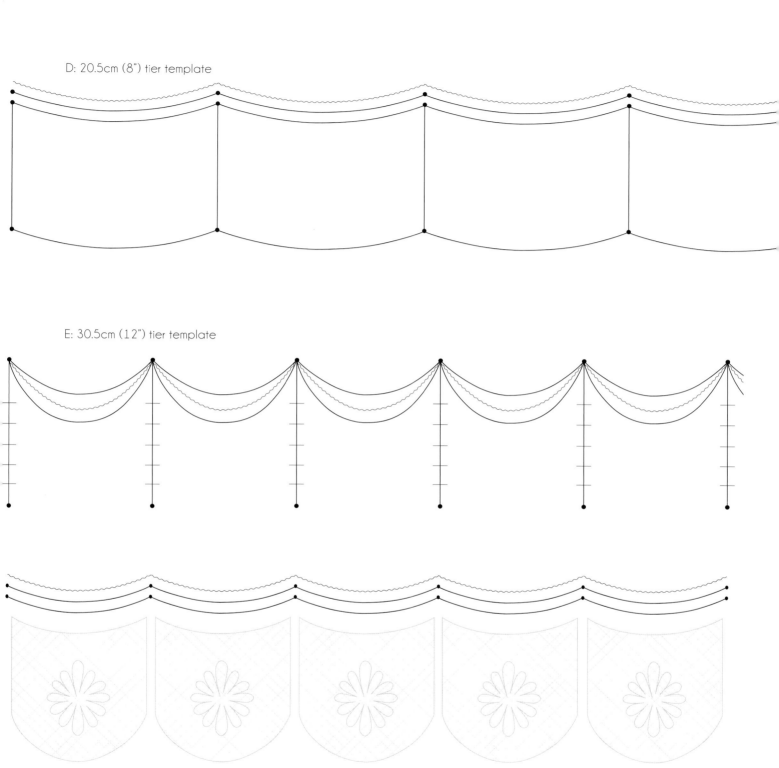

$\mathscr{S}$UPPLIERS

Squires Kitchen, UK
3 Waverley Lane
Farnham
Surrey
GU9 8BB
0845 61 71 810
+44 (0) 1252 260 260
www.squires-shop.com

Squires Kitchen International School, UK
The Grange
Hones Yard
Farnham
Surrey
GU9 8BB
0845 61 71 810
+44 (0) 1252 260 260
www.squires-school.co.uk

Distributors

UK

Culpitt Ltd.
Northumberland
www.culpitt.com

Guy, Paul & Co. Ltd.
Buckinghamshire
www.guypaul.co.uk

Squires Kitchen
Surrey
www.squires-shop.com

For your nearest sugarcraft supplier, please contact your local distributor.

Europe

Cake Supplies
Netherlands
www.cakesupplies.nl

Dom Konditera LLC
Belarus/Russia
www.domkonditera.com

Sugar World – Aliprantis Ltd.
Greece
www.sugarworld.gr

Tårtdecor
Sweden
www.tartdecor.se

 B. Dutton Publishing is an award-winning publisher of cake decorating titles. To find out more about our books, follow us at **www.facebook.com/bduttonpublishing**.

BELLISSIMO FLEXI SMOOTHERS

Bellissimo Flexi Smoothers are designed to help you achieve sharp, clean edges on all your sugarpasted cakes. With one rounded and one straight-edged smoother, Bellissimo Flexi Smoothers allow you to create perfectly crisp edges easily for a clean, polished and professional finish. Bellissimo Flexi Smoothers are available from all good cake decorating suppliers.